30223 ISS   QR
NYC

The Media

ISSUES

Volume 210

Series Editor

Lisa Firth

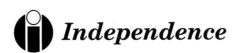

Independence

Educational Publishers

Cambridge

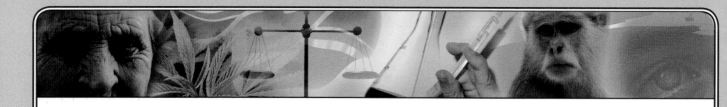

First published by Independence

The Studio, High Green

Great Shelford

Cambridge CB22 5EG

England

© Independence 2011

British Library Cataloguing in Publication Data

The media. -- (Issues ; v. 210)

1. Mass media--Social aspects.

I. Series II. Firth, Lisa.

302.2'3-dc22

ISBN-13: 978 1 86168 586 5

Printed in Great Britain

MWL Print Group Ltd

Chapter 1 Media Trends

Chapter 2 New Media

Chapter 3 Regulations and Privacy

OTHER TITLES IN THE ISSUES SERIES

For more on these titles, visit: www.independence.co.uk

A note on critical evaluation

Because the information reprinted here is from a number of different sources, readers should bear in mind the origin of the text and whether the source is likely to have a particular bias when presenting information (just as they would if undertaking their own research). It is hoped that, as you read about the many aspects of the issues explored in this book, you will critically evaluate the information presented. It is important that you decide whether you are being presented with facts or opinions. Does the writer give a biased or an unbiased report? If an opinion is being expressed, do you agree with the writer?

The Media offers a useful starting point for those who need convenient access to information about the many issues involved. However, it is only a starting point. Following each article is a URL to the relevant organisation's website, which you may wish to visit for further information.

The UK's media landscape

Information from the European Journalism Centre.

Introduction

The media landscape in the United Kingdom is large, complex and mature, arguably ranking second globally to that of the USA. This status is derived to some extent from the use of English as the primary natural language of production and content. Although none of the major global media conglomerates is based in the UK, a number of media organisations, notably Reuters and the BBC, have international standing in their own right. UK activities also contribute significantly to the operations of global conglomerates, such as NewsCorp, Bertelsmann and Time Warner. A desire to be present in emerging global media markets led to increasing deregulation under both Conservative and Labour governments since 1979.

> **The UK is effectively saturated with traditional electronic media; multi-television, multi-radio and multi-telephone households are commonplace**

The UK media sector is relatively open, with participants from many countries active in almost all aspects – newspapers, television, magazines, radio, film, books, advertising, music, telephones and public relations. At the same time, UK media organisations have interests in many parts of the world. Since the late 1990s, successive Labour governments have attempted to elide the distinction between culture and commerce, leading to the adoption of the idea of the 'creative industries'. The UK has also been affected by the general decline in consumption of traditional media, particularly newspapers, which has been evident in most developed countries. The government objective is for the UK to be digital by 2014. These trends have been accompanied by widespread and vociferous concerns about media quality.

It should be remembered that, while, in many respects, the UK media landscape is a single entity, there are distinctive English, Scottish, Irish and Welsh dimensions, reflecting the composition of the State itself, and

heightened by political and administrative devolution in the late 1990s. The UK's adult population numbers 47.5 million, and the total population is 61 million.

Traditional media

The UK is effectively saturated with traditional electronic media: multi-television, multi-radio and multi-telephone households are commonplace. The four sectors are worth a total of about 100 billion British pounds (111 million euro) a year. The audiovisual media's major defining characteristic is the existence of a strong public service broadcaster, the BBC, supported by a universal compulsory television licence fee.

Print media

Perhaps the most distinguishing characteristic of the print media is the existence of a large national newspaper sector, comprised of 11 daily and the same number of Sunday titles. (The numbers include two Scottish papers, the *Daily Record* and *Sunday Mail*.) About 75 million such papers are sold every week, which are read by about 70 per cent of the adult population. In July 2009, the total sales of national newspapers were just under 11 million for both daily and Sunday titles. These numbers were well below peaks reached in the late 1950s. The last half-century has been one of secular decline in national newspaper sales and readerships.

In 2009, sales of national daily newspapers were 2.25 per cent below 2008 figures, and sales of Sunday titles had fallen by 4 per cent. Such was the state of circulation decline that in 2009 the owners, Guardian Media, were actively considering closing *The Observer* (398,000), the world's oldest Sunday newspaper. Closure of *The Independent* (198,000) and *The Independent on Sunday* (160,000) was also being canvassed.

This press is commonly divided into three sectors – 'quality', 'middle market' and 'red-top tabloid'. For more than 20 years, all the papers in the latter two categories have been tabloid in size. More recently, three of the 'quality' titles abandoned the broadsheet format and adopted either a 'compact' (*The Independent* and *The Times*) or Berliner (*The Guardian*) size. This change stimulated much debate over whether the national press was abandoning 'serious' journalism.

The entire national newspaper press is owned by eight companies, of which the largest two (News International and Daily Mail and General Trust) had 55 per cent of market share in 2005. With Trinity Mirror (16 per cent) and Northern and Shell (14.5 per cent), the top four owners control 85 per cent of the market.

A similar concentration of ownership is evident in the regional and local press. The five largest owners control 72.5 per cent of the market – more than 700 newspapers. Of those, three (Trinity Mirror, Associated and Northcliffe) are also among the top four national newspaper companies. In sum, then, all forms of newspaper ownership are heavily concentrated in three corporations (News International, Trinity Mirror and Daily Mail and General Trust/Northcliffe/Associated), amounting to 360 titles (28 per cent of all newspapers in the UK), some of them the largest circulating in their sectors.

There are estimated to be 1,250 Sunday, week-day (morning and evening) and weekly (sometimes twice weekly) regional and local titles, further sub-divided between those papers which charge a cover price and those which are distributed for free. In all, around 40 million copies of regional and local newspapers circulate and are read by about 84 per cent of the adult population. More than 90 per cent circulate once (occasionally, twice) a week. Individual readerships are on the whole small.

The much smaller numbers of regional and local daily (25 morning and 75 evening) and Sunday (21) titles generally have larger circulations. This is the layer at which a distinctive press serving England (particularly London), Scotland, Wales and Northern Ireland is most evident. The biggest selling regional and local papers are published in Scotland.

The regional and local press has suffered long-term decline. In the 1960s, evening newspapers were read in nine out of ten households in their circulation areas. In 2006, many commentators believed they would soon cease to exist. Between 2008 and 2009, all regional daily newspapers (morning and evening) lost circulation, with falls of up to 18.4 per cent. The *London Evening Standard*, until recently the largest selling evening newspaper in the UK, was sold for a nominal sum, and in 2009 it was selling only 144,260 copies, an effective fall of 20 per cent on 2008.

Attempts to attract readers with alternative formats began in 1999 when Associated Newspapers launched the free commuter paper *Metro* in London. By 2003, total distributions of a series of *Metro* titles in British cities totalled 840,000, making it the world's largest free newspaper. In response, some paid-for papers, such as

the *Evening Standard* and *Manchester Evening News*, started free 'lite' editions. In September 2006, News International (owned by NewsCorp) launched the free *London Paper* in competition with the Standard's *London Lite*. Many of these titles have since ceased publication, including the *London Paper* which closed in 2009.

A number of regional dailies switched, or were on the verge of switching, to weekly publication. In addition, more than 50 local papers (mostly freesheets) closed in 2008.

Newspaper advertising revenues have also been falling steadily since 2004. The rate of decline (five per cent a year) has been five times as great in the regional and local press as it has in the national press. Newspapers account for about 25 per cent of all advertising.

The UK magazine sector is also large and was growing for more than a decade. There are between 8,800 and 10,000 titles (estimates vary). About two-thirds are 'business and professional' titles, and the rest are 'consumer' magazines. The former often have very small controlled circulations (mostly on subscription), while best-selling consumer titles have readerships of one million or more. Neither the very biggest selling titles, nor most of the business and professional periodicals, are normally sold through news-stands. Nevertheless, the consumer magazines which are sold this way are the most visible part of the sector.

News-stand sales of about 300 consumer magazine titles account for around 100 million copies each month.

EUROPEAN JOURNALISM CENTRE

Only two magazines sold over the counter, *What's On TV* (1.2 million) and *TV Choice* (1.3 million), are among those with the largest circulations. The others are 'customer' or 'member' magazines, produced for mainly free distribution as marketing tools.

Although there are almost 1,000 magazine publishers, as with the newspaper industry, there are also heavy concentrations of ownership. Only 25 are considered to be major players, but since the late 1990s the larger companies have been reducing their relative shares of the market. Unlike the newspaper industry, the magazine sector has a number of major European owners, such as H Bauer and Hachette Filipacchi.

The BBC attracts about a third of the total TV audience

Consumer magazine circulations have been falling, too, by as much as 25 per cent. The largest seven publishers, which control circulations aggregating to about 21 million, lost sales in 2009: Hachette Filipacchi (-6 per cent); National Magazine Company (-4.3 per cent); Condé Nast (-5.8 per cent); IPC Media (-8.9 per cent); Bauer Media (-6.1 per cent); BBC Worldwide (-8.5 per cent) and H Bauer (-4.9 per cent).

Finally, it is worth noting that there are substantial 'minority' and 'alternative' press sectors in the UK. These address a wide range of cultural, ethnic, linguistic, religious, lifestyle, political, environmental and social areas.

Radio

Radio has enjoyed a recent resurgence in popularity. More than 90 per cent of people over 15 years of age (46.3 million) listen at least once a week. However, it is national, rather than local, stations which have increased their popularity.

The BBC operates ten national radio stations; the World Service; regional stations in Scotland, Wales and Northern Ireland (including stations broadcasting in Welsh and Scots), and 30 local stations. Radio is also characterised by a multi-faceted commercial presence alongside that of the BBC. About 300 commercial radio stations broadcast across a number of platforms, the vast majority being local.

In mid-2009, the BBC's overall share of the radio audience was 54.6 per cent: commercial radio had 42.7 per cent. The BBC's Radio 2 had the largest single station weekly reach (13.42 million listeners). Radio 1 reached 11.45 million people. Classic FM, the largest single commercial station, reached 5.4 million. On the other hand, the reach of local commercial radio is greater

than that of local BBC services. The largest commercial radio group, Global Radio, with 33 stations, claims about 40 per cent of all commercial radio listening (19 million listeners). A small number of large chains dominates the sector. These include Bauer Radio (12.65 million listeners) and GMG (5 million). However, commercial radio advertising revenues have been declining since 2003. They account for about 2.8 per cent of total display advertising.

There are also more than 205 community radio licences, with more than 140 community stations on air.

Television

UK television channels broadcast about 2.5 million hours of programming a year. There are four main public service free-to-air broadcasters (the BBC [operating two services, One and Two], Independent Television [ITV], Channel 4 and 5) which attract about 60 per cent of total viewing. Three of these (ITV, Channel 4 and 5) carry advertising. UK television is also characterised by multi-channel provision, much of it subscription based, although the BBC has eight channels.

More than 90 per cent of UK households have multi-channel television. Nearly 500 channels are available (including 30 24/7 news channels). BSkyB, controlled by NewsCorp, is the major satellite provider. Freeview is a set-top box system jointly owned by the BBC, BSkyB and Crown Castle. Sky operates 26 channels of its own, including nine movie channels and five sports channels. Others available include those from the BBC, ITV, Channel 4 and 5, plus global offerings such as Cartoon Network, CNN, Discovery, DW-TV, Fox News, MTV, Nickelodeon, TCM and VH1.

Ironically, the public service broadcasters have been leading the charge into multi-channel services. The BBC operates 14 television channels globally. A number of commercial multi-channel services have recently been withdrawn or cut back, the most notable of which was the closure of the UK business of Setanta Sports.

In all, the BBC attracts about a third of the total TV audience. It is funded through the collection of a universal licence fee (in 2009, £142.50). The main free-to-air commercial public service broadcaster, ITV, has about a 25 per cent share, and the rest is shared across many channels.

Television accounts for about 23 per cent of the UK's display advertising market.

8 November 2010

⇨ The above information is reprinted with kind permission from the European Journalism Centre. Visit www.ejc.net for more information.

© *European Journalism Centre*

EUROPEAN JOURNALISM CENTRE

Media and communication trends

The IPA has today (22 July 2010) revealed the results of its third IPA TouchPoints Hub Survey, which describes a week in the life of a representative sample of the GB adult population during late 2009/early 2010.

Key findings

People watch 3.7 hours of television per day, listen to the radio for 2.1 hours and access the Internet for 1.8 hours per day. The time people spend on the Internet has increased by 38% in the past two years, 37% of adults claim to social network each week, and the time spent writing to someone on paper has fallen to just 1% of communication time.

The IPA TouchPoints Survey is one of the most ambitious pieces of media research ever undertaken. It provides communication strategists with a consumer-centric planning tool which analyses how people are using the increasingly wide range of media available to them and how this usage fits in to their lifestyles.

IPA TouchPoints3, which has been conducted by Ipsos MediaCT, has been extensively updated and expanded, particularly in its coverage of digital media (including mobile, VOD, social networking), and with the addition of word-of-mouth and gaming. It also provides a range of trend data where comparisons with IPA TouchPoints1 (launched in 2006) and 2 (launched in 2008) are possible.

The IPA TouchPoints Database is extremely extensive, covering general life activities, attitudes and media usage. Insights include the following:

How people are communicating

⇨ Of the time they spend communicating, adults spend 75% talking or chatting face-to-face. This percentage share has fallen from 77% in 2008 and 81% in 2006. The share spent on the phone – landline or mobile – has stayed relatively constant at 11% whilst SMS texting and picture messaging has grown to a 4% share. The time spent writing to someone on paper has fallen to just 1% of communication time.

⇨ For 15-24s, 72% of their communication time is spent on face-to-face talking/chatting, down from 75% in TouchPoints2. 15-24s' area of largest growth is SMS texting and picture messaging which now takes a 9% share of their time compared to 6% two years ago.

Overall media trends

⇨ Television remains the dominant medium for all adults in terms of average hours consumed per day (3.7) (weekly reach 98%), followed by out-of-home (2.3 hours/99% reach), radio (2.1 hours/89% reach) and then Internet (1.8 hours/75% reach).

⇨ About the same number of adults use a mobile phone (57%) as read a newspaper (59%) each week and for a similar amount of time; whilst just less than 40% of adults indulge in social networking each week for about an hour.

⇨ Watching TV online and watching video online is done by just less than 20% of adults each week for about a quarter-of-an-hour a day.

⇨ Only minor changes in the levels of television viewing (-5%), radio listening (+1%) and reading (-5%) have been recorded since 2008. Any marginal decline in consuming each medium through traditional means have been more than compensated for by the growth in their consumption through their digital platforms.

⇨ The only medium to record a significant increase in audience is online, with hours spent using the Internet on an average day up from 1.3 to 1.8 hours – a 38% increase.

⇨ The number of adults using more than one medium in any half-hourly period has increased from 74% to 75%; for 15-24s the growth has been from 75% to 78%.

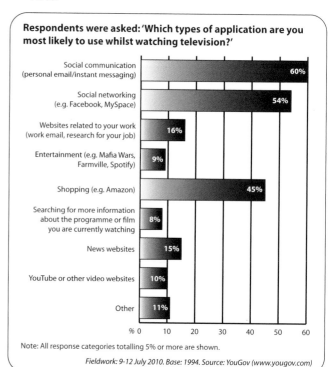

Respondents were asked: 'Which types of application are you most likely to use whilst watching television?'

Application	%
Social communication (personal email/instant messaging)	60%
Social networking (e.g. Facebook, MySpace)	54%
Websites related to your work (work email, research for your job)	16%
Entertainment (e.g. Mafia Wars, Farmville, Spotify)	9%
Shopping (e.g. Amazon)	45%
Searching for more information about the programme or film you are currently watching	8%
News websites	15%
YouTube or other video websites	10%
Other	11%

Note: All response categories totalling 5% or more are shown.

Fieldwork: 9-12 July 2010. Base: 1994. Source: YouGov (www.yougov.com)

For 15-24s, television is still the largest overall medium (97% weekly reach/2.6 average daily hours) but Internet use (96%/2.3 hours) is a very close second with out-of-home third (99%/2.2 hours). The reach and average time spent by 15-24s talking on a mobile phone, watching video online and watching

The BBC continues to be the dominant supplier of media to the British public

television is greater than for all adults, whilst the time spent reading newspapers and magazines falls in comparison to all adults.

The BBC continues to be the dominant supplier of media to the British public. It reaches 98% of all adults with at least one of its television, radio, online and magazine properties. In comparison, Sky only reaches about half that number.

Digital trends

The percentage of adults claiming to use the Internet in a week now stands at 75% rising from 53% in TouchPoints2.

The daily amount of time spent using the Internet has shown a significant 38% increase in the same period, up from 1.3 hours to 1.8 hours. This increase in usage has occurred throughout the day but is relatively greater in the evening and is being primarily driven by the growth in social networking.

The growth in Internet usage has been across all age groups but is relatively larger for 15-24s, i.e. +43% compared to 20% growth amongst those aged 55+.

Usage of the Internet in general has a slight male bias and is more heavily biased towards ABC1s and of course, under-54s. It also has a quite marked regional bias towards London and the South East with the rest of the country being much lighter Internet users of all types.

The incidence of using the Internet and watching the television at the same time is highest between 7pm and 9pm.

Emailing is still the dominant Internet activity, accounting for a 20% share of all Internet activity. The next largest activity is using the Internet for work, which takes a 16% share. Both activities have shown substantial growth in overall time use; however, due to the even more rapid growths in other activities they have lost overall share between surveys. The time spent social networking has risen by 113%

therefore increasing its share of Internet activity to 11%. Although, still at the 1-2% share levels, the time spent consuming media online has also grown substantially; listening to radio/podcasts is up by 166%, looking at newspaper websites by 61% and watching online television by 216%.

16% of all adults and 34% of 15-24s use their mobile phones to access the Internet each week.

Social media trends

37% of adults claim to social network each week – as we know, this group is particularly skewed towards 15-34s, particularly 15-24s, and those either still studying or working full-time and also has a slight female and ABC1 bias. The incidence of social networking also has a strong regional bias towards London and the South East: with the notable exception of the North West, the rest of the country are much lighter social networkers.

35% of all adults claim to use Facebook each week – up from 16% in 2008

Social networking takes place throughout the whole day but peak time for people to social network is between 6.30pm and 10pm in the evening when 3 to 3.5% of adults claim to be active – about a third of these also claim to be watching the television at the same time. Only a relatively low level of people claim to be social networking at work and this peaks over lunchtime.

35% of all adults claim to use Facebook each week – up from 16% in 2008. For 15-24s, Facebook's weekly reach is 79% – up from 39% in 2008.

Only 4% of adults claim to use Twitter once a week or more whilst the comparative weekly reach figure for Linkedin is 1.4%.

22 July 2010

Note

The survey, conducted by Ipsos MediaCT, questioned 6,050 adults aged 15+ through a substantial self-completion questionnaire and an e-diary that collected data every half hour for a week on how they were spending their time, their opinions, and the role of media in their lives.

The extract above is reprinted with kind permission from IPA. Visit www.ipa.co.uk for more information.

© IPA

IPA

Who makes the news?

Only 24% of news subjects (the people in the news) are female.

The Global Media Monitoring Project

The Global Media Monitoring Project (GMMP) maps the representation of women and men in news media worldwide. GMMP research has been carried out in five-year cycles since 1995 and relies on the voluntary efforts of hundreds of individuals and organisations, including grassroots communication groups, media professionals and university researchers.

The 1995, 2000 and 2005 studies revealed that women are grossly under-represented in news coverage in contrast to men. The outcome of under-representation is an imbalanced picture of the world, one in which women are largely absent. The studies equally showed a paucity of women's voices in news media content in contrast to men's perspectives, resulting in news that presents a male-centred view of the world. On 10 November 2009, 1,281 newspapers, television and radio stations were monitored in 108 countries for the fourth GMMP. The research covered 16,734 news items, 20,769 news personnel (announcers, presenters and reporters) and 35,543 total news subjects.

Internet news monitoring was introduced on a pilot basis for the first time in the GMMP. 76 national news websites in 16 countries and eight international news websites containing 1,061 news items, 2,710 news subjects and 1,044 news personnel were studied.

The following summary outlines key findings.

News subjects

⇨ Only 24% of the people heard or read about in print, radio and television news are female. In contrast, 76% – more than three out of four – of the people in the news are male. This is a significant improvement from 1995 when only 17% of the people in the news were women. However, despite a slow but overall steady increase in women's presence in the news over the past ten years, the world depicted in the news remains predominantly male. This picture is incongruent with a reality in which at least one half of the world's population is female.

⇨ News continue to portray a world in which men outnumber women in almost all occupational categories, the highest disparity being in the professions. The proportion of female news subjects identified, represented or portrayed as workers or professionals over the past ten years has risen in some occupational categories. The gap, however, remains high, especially in the professions as depicted in the news. Further, out of 25 occupational categories, women outnumber men in only two: news subjects presented as homemakers (72%) and those presented as students (54%). The picture seen through the news becomes one of a world where women are virtually invisible as active participants in work outside the home.

⇨ As persons interviewed or heard in the news, women remain lodged in the 'ordinary' people categories, in contrast to men who continue to predominate in the 'expert' categories. Women are inching closer to parity as people providing popular opinion in the news, at 44% of persons interviewed in the news in this capacity compared to 34% in 2005. Despite the gains, only 19% of spokespersons and 20% of experts are women. In contrast, 81% of spokespersons and 80% of experts in the news are male.

⇨ 18% of female news subjects are portrayed as victims in comparison to 8% of male subjects. In contrast, women are now twice as likely to be portrayed as survivors than men. While the gap between the percentage of women and the percentage of men depicted as victims remains large, it has been narrowing gradually since 1995. Remarkably, in 2010, 6% of females in contrast to 3% of males are portrayed as survivors. This is a reversal of the situation in 2005 when 4% of females compared to 8% of males were portrayed as survivors.

Reporters and presenters

⇨ For stories reported on television, radio and newspapers, the percentage of those by female reporters is exactly similar to that registered in 2005; that is, 37%. The percentage of stories by female reporters across all three mediums combined rose until 2005. The statistics for radio are noteworthy for the sharp rise between 2000 and 2005 (from 27% to 45% of stories reported by women), followed by a dramatic eight percentage point drop five years later. The negative change on radio between 2005 and 2010 accounts for the stagnation in the overall average statistic found in 2010.

⇨ 52% of stories on television and 45% of those on radio are presented by women. The average total number of stories on television and radio presented by women is 49%, less than half of the total number of stories on both mediums combined, a four percentage point drop since 2005 and lower than in 1995 when the statistic was 51%.

52% of stories on television and 45% of those on radio are presented by women

⇨ Since the year 2000, the percentage of stories reported by women compared to those reported by men has increased in all major topics except science/health. Nonetheless, stories by male reporters continue to exceed those by female reporters in all topics. The changes range from three to 11 percentage points, the highest increase being in stories on celebrity/arts. Men report 67% of stories on politics/government, 65% of stories on crime/violence and 60% of stories on the economy. The percentage of stories on science/health reported by women declined sharply between 2000 and 2005 from 46% to 38%, a decline that was followed by an increase to 44% in 2010 that nevertheless has not been sufficient to bring the proportion back up to the level noted a decade ago.

⇨ Stories by female reporters contain more female news subjects than stories by male reporters. This trend has persisted over the past ten years. In 2000, 24% of news subjects in stories by female reporters were female, in contrast to only 18% in stories by male reporters. Currently, the statistics stand at 28% and 22%, respectively.

News content

⇨ 13% of all stories focus specifically on women. This is a statistically significant change from the 10% found in the 2005 research. In the major topic politics/

government women are now central in 13% of stories compared to 8% in 2005; in science/health it went from 6% in 2005 to 16% in 2010; and in stories on economy from 3% to 11%.

⇨ Only 6% of stories highlight issues of gender equality or inequality. The major topics science/health and social/legal contain higher proportions of stories that highlight (in)equality issues, than topics in which women have historically been marginalised, namely those on politics and the economy. The latter are topics that dominate the news agenda.

⇨ 46% of stories reinforce gender stereotypes, almost eight times higher than stories that challenge such stereotypes (6%). Over 50% of stories on crime reinforce stereotypes, followed closely by celebrity and political stories. Of all the topics, social/legal stories most often challenge stereotypes than stories on any other topic.

⇨ Stories by female reporters are visibly more likely to challenge stereotypes than those filed by male reporters and are also less likely to reinforce stereotypes than those reported by men. 7% of stories reported by women challenge stereotypes, in contrast to 4% of stories by male reporters. 35% of stories by female reporters reinforce stereotypes compared to 42% of stories reported by men. These statistics evidence sex disparity in reporting patterns on this indicator.

⇨ Only 10% of stories quote or refer to relevant local, national, regional or international legal instruments on gender equality and/or human rights. This

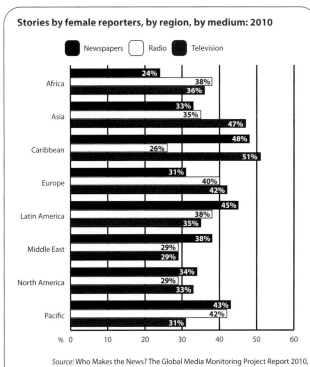

Stories by female reporters, by region, by medium: 2010

■ Newspapers □ Radio ■ Television

Africa: 24%, 38%, 36%
Asia: 33%, 35%, 47%
Caribbean: 48%, 26%, 51%
Europe: 31%, 40%, 42%
Latin America: 45%, 38%, 35%
Middle East: 38%, 29%, 29%
North America: 34%, 29%, 33%
Pacific: 43%, 42%, 31%

Source: Who Makes the News? The Global Media Monitoring Project Report 2010,
© *World Association for Christian Communication: www.whomakesthenews.org*

WORLD ASSOCIATION FOR CHRISTIAN COMMUNICATION

finding suggests that numerous stories miss the opportunity to create awareness on instruments enacted to protect human rights, women's rights or gender equality, supporting an observation by gender and communication groups on the relative invisibility of human/women's rights in mainstream news content.

Internet news

➩ Women comprised only 23% of the news subjects in stories from the 84 news websites monitored. This finding suggests that the under-representation of women in traditional news media has been carried over into the virtual news world.

➩ 16% of female online news subjects were depicted as victims in contrast to 5% of the male news subjects.

➩ Only 36% of the news stories in the sample were reported by women, compared to 64% of stories by men.

➩ 42% of the online news stories were found to reinforce gender stereotypes, only 4% challenged them, and the majority, 54%, neither reinforced nor challenged stereotypes. Overall, the differences, some of which are statistically significant, point to a conclusion that Internet news is a format in which gender biases become not only more visible but even more concentrated than in the traditional news media.

➩ The above information is reprinted with kind permission from the World Association for Christian Communication's Global Media Monitoring Project website *Who Makes the News?* Visit www.whomakesthenews.org for more.

© *World Association for Christian Communication 2010*

Negative effects of media/entertainment upon teens

Information from Child.net.

It seems that more often than not, the media/entertainment industry is portrayed in a negative way for teens based on the influence that it has. It can influence teens both positively and negatively, and can result in the formation of specific habits and establishment of norms.

How media shapes teen habits

Let's face it, in most cases the media/entertainment industry isn't getting you outside and moving around. You're most likely to bunker down in front of the TV for a favourite show or to play a video game. You're still sedentary even while doing something positive like reading a newspaper or magazine. With these norms, you're more likely to stay inside versus getting yourself out there and active during your teenage years, and that's not always a good thing if you're lacking balance.

How entertainment shapes teen norms

Things you see on TV and in the media help align what you believe to be the norms. Whether you're watching violence, looking at an extremely skinny model in a magazine, or something else entirely, the things that you see are the things you expect to be normal. While you might be able to use your judgment, in some circumstances, the media is establishing right from wrong, and that can get you in trouble as a teen!

Positive effects of media on teens

The positive effects of the media might not be touched upon often, but they do exist. Teens can learn from media and entertainment, develop new skills, and stay out of trouble as well.

Learning from media

Teens can learn from reading newspapers, magazines and even from watching movies. Through these mediums you gain information about current and historical events and become informed about things you might not otherwise have been aware of. As long as you make smart choices about what you're seeing and how you choose to interpret it, there is no harm! If your parents talk to you about media influences, remember to accept what they're saying as looking out for your best interest.

Media/entertainment and staying out of trouble

It can be argued that as you're glued to your TV or video game (two of the more criticised mediums), that you're not doing yourself any favours as a teen. Well, you're better off there than on the streets getting involved in crime, so it's not all that bad. Just remember to do everything in moderation!

➩ The above information is reprinted with kind permission from Child.net. Visit www.child.net for more information.

© *Child.net*

Real life vs reality TV

A unique insight into human behaviour or stage-managed humiliation? Laura Bond examines our national obsession with reality TV.

Who hasn't raced home to watch a *Big Brother* eviction, *The Apprentice* or a bit of *Katie & Alex*? Diving into someone else's life for half an hour can provoke a range of emotions and experiences that the daily grind fails to deliver. We witness a world full of passionate embraces, cunning deception and characters teetering on the brink of radical change or chaos.

Initially dismissed by media experts as a passing fad, reality TV now dominates the schedules. *Morecambe And Wise* or *The Generation Game* were once the modern fireplace around which the family gathered, but now it's *Strictly Come Dancing* or *The X Factor*. More than nine million viewers tuned in to the *Strictly* Christmas special, a significant figure in our multi-channel world.

Behavioural insight

It has been criticised for dumbing down its audience, but reality TV is undeniably informative. It can bring culture to millions (*Clash Of The Choirs*), break down prejudice towards mental illness (*How Mad Are You?*) and provide an insight into human behaviour. But whether you enjoy it or can't stand it, reality TV has entered the collective mindset and affects all of us more than we may realise – with some worrying implications.

Pioneering reality shows, such as the 1970s' classic *The Family*, were relatively innocent documentaries of human life. But now producers have become much more involved in guiding what contestants say or do. Stuart Murphy, creative director of Twofour Broadcast, has been producing reality TV for the past decade, including recent hits such as *Make My Body Younger*. 'Viewers were once quite happy watching not much happen,' says Murphy. 'But audiences now demand more from reality TV.'

Manufactured emotions

Moments of shock, awe and devastation are packed into bite-size episodes of reality TV. But these dramatic scenes are often far from organic. 'One of the things you learn in this industry is how to shock your audience,' says Murphy. 'If you genuinely shock someone, they will just look slightly traumatised. So producers gently prepare the characters for revelations so they respond in a TV-friendly way.'

Murphy admits that reality TV is cheaper to produce than soaps or dramas, but insists this is not the main reason for the glut of reality shows. 'Reality shows can also help us manage our emotions. When we see real people behaving in unexpected, contradictory ways it can make us more comfortable with our own complicated natures.'

But does reality TV also make us more comfortable with losing our temper or ridiculing others? The term 'humilitainment' was coined by media psychologists to describe the tendency for viewers to be attracted to scenes of humiliation or mortification, for example bullying, nudity and drunken antics.

According to psychology professor Dr Douglas Gentile, one worrying effect of reality TV is that it might make us more aggressive. Gentile released a study revealing that those who watch more indirect aggression on TV – such as gossiping, eye-rolling or making sarcastic comments – behave more aggressively. The study also highlights that when aggression is perceived to be more realistic, it has a bigger influence on the viewer.

Body issues

Many people look to television as a guide to what is ideal, and the plastic-surgery makeover genre is becoming increasingly popular. Dr Julie Albright, Professor of Psychology at the University of Southern California, has completed a study revealing that women who watch plastic-surgery reality shows are more anxious about their bodies and more likely to see their 'problem' body parts as a moral failing.

While viewers may be savvy enough to realise that 'real life' shows are only loosely based on a true story, the more we watch TV, the more tempted we become to believe in the world it represents. But while TV prefers the visual impact of primary colours, the real world is shaded with a more complex palette.

Ultimately, we have a responsibility for what appears on our screens – if we didn't watch reality shows, broadcasters wouldn't commission them. So while we continue to tune in, we should remember that in real life there is no diary room to repent in, should we lash out at a loved one. It may also be useful to switch channels more often. 'We might now look to comedy or drama to see the genuinely ordinary,' says Murphy. 'You can't depend on reality TV to provide that anymore.'

⇨ The above information is reprinted with kind permission from Psychologies. Visit www.psychologies.co.uk for more information.

© Psychologies

TV, phones and Internet take up almost half of our waking hours

UK consumers are spending almost half (45 per cent) of their waking hours watching TV, using their mobiles and other communications devices, new Ofcom research reveals today.

We're now sending four times as many texts per day as in 2004, spending almost a quarter of our Internet time on social networking sites and spending three hours and 45 minutes per day watching TV.

We're also using several types of media at the same time – with the average person cramming eight hours 48 minutes of media into just over seven hours during the average day.

The growing popularity of smartphones – and the changing way we use our mobiles – is increasing our overall use of communications, and helping us do much more simultaneously.

This is being particularly driven by the under-25s, although the over-55s are catching up, with half now having broadband at home – the fastest growing age group.

Communication fast facts 2010

⇨ 89 per cent have or use a mobile phone.

⇨ 92 per cent of UK homes have digital TV.

⇨ 14 per cent live in a mobile-only household.

⇨ A record 104 billion texts were sent in 2009. That works out as 1700 texts for every person in the UK.

⇨ Time spent on fixed Internet has increased by over two-thirds since 2008.

⇨ Adults now spend 14.2 hours per month on the web.

⇨ 15 per cent of UK adults have mobile broadband.

⇨ Take-up of mobile broadband increased by eight per cent among 15 to 24s and by three per cent among 35 to 54s.

⇨ Data volumes over mobile networks increased by 240 per cent in 2009.

⇨ A record number of people listened to the radio – 46.5 million adults listened on a weekly basis by the first quarter of 2010.

More for less

But while we are doing more, it is costing us less.

For the fifth year in a row, our spending on communications services has decreased.

Ofcom's annual *Communications Market Report* into the UK's TV, radio, telecoms and Internet industries shows that real household monthly spend on communication services fell 9.4 per cent over the past five years to £91.24, as more people choose to buy their services in discounted bundles.

Men spend nearly an hour more per day using media than women – an average of seven hours 33 minutes per day compared with six hours 38 minutes

The report also shows that traditional media is far from dead, with TV retaining a central part in our lives, particularly in the evening.

Communications services

Peter Phillips, Ofcom Partner, Strategy & Market Developments, said: 'For the first time we can see just how central media and communications are to our lives – on average we use them for nearly half our waking hours.

'Increasingly, mobile devices – especially smartphones – are used for multi-media, but live evening TV still remains the main entertainment event of the day.

'Younger people have shown the biggest changes in how we use media – particularly using different media at the same time.

'But the divide between younger and older people's use of technology is starting to narrow as more older people are getting online and finding that things like email are very important to them.

'Consumers are using communications services more – phone calls, texting and the Internet. Yet they are paying less despite getting more, partly through buying in bundles.'

OFCOM

A more in-depth look at how we're using our communications in 2010 follows.

Mobiles, smartphones and media multi-tasking

Media multi-tasking – where, for example, you make a phone call while surfing the Internet – now accounts for one-fifth of all media consumed throughout the day – and the younger the person, the more this happens.

Ofcom's research found that:

⇨ Among 16-24s, almost a third (29 per cent) of their media activity is simultaneous, compared to just over one-eighth (12 per cent) for people aged over 55;

⇨ UK consumers are now generally using a single device – typically their mobile phone – for more than one type of media and communications use;

⇨ There has also been a surge in smartphone ownership – up 81 per cent from 7.2 million users in May 2009 to 12.8 million in May 2010;

⇨ In June 2010, over a quarter of people in the UK (26.5 per cent) said they had a smartphone, more than double the number two years previously;

⇨ In the first three months of 2010 nearly a quarter of adults (23 per cent) accessed content or sent emails on their mobile phones – among 15-24s this rises to 45 per cent;

⇨ Surfing the Internet via mobile phones is the fastest growing mobile media activity with one million new users during the first quarter of 2010 (taking the total to 13.5 million, compared to nine million in the first quarter of 2009);

⇨ A fifth (20 per cent) of the time 16-24s spend social networking is on a mobile;

⇨ In the second quarter of 2010, 63 per cent of new mobile contracts were for 24 months, compared to just three per cent in the second quarter of 2008, making smartphones more affordable for consumers as costs are spread over a longer period of time.

Consumers still attached to their TVs and radio

Although media multi-tasking is widespread, half of people consume only one type of media in the evening.

This peak-time evening media use is driven by people watching scheduled live television through their TV set, an activity mainly undertaken on its own rather than with other media.

The time people spend watching TV remains stable, with the average person watching three hours and 45 minutes of TV per day.

And despite the growing choice in technology and services available, watching TV remains the activity that most adults would miss the most.

Compared to 2007, a growing number of 16-24s (eight percentage points) and over-55s (seven percentage points) say that watching TV is the activity they would miss the most.

Five million households have now also signed up to HD services

---

Catch-up TV usage grows

It's not just scheduled live television which continues to be popular. Ofcom's consumer research from the first quarter of 2010 shows that almost a third of households with Internet access used it to watch online catch-up TV – up eight per cent over the year.

Nearly a quarter of people (22 per cent) say they have bought a HD-ready TV set in the last 12 months and sales of HD-ready TV sets have now passed 24 million in the UK.

Five million households have now also signed up to HD services through pay TV, freesat and Freeview services.

Although the continuing demand for TVs could be partly explained by falling prices and digital switchover, it also suggests that consumers are as attached to their TVs as they ever were and are hungry for more channels and better picture quality.

It also highlights the potential for fast growth of other services through TV sets, such as Internet, or of new technologies such as 3DTV.

Younger and older people embracing technology but in different ways

Ofcom's research found that 16-24s are the most efficient users of communications services, squeezing 9.5 hours of media consumption into just over 6.5 hours actual time and spending the largest part of this time on computers and mobiles.

Over two-thirds (67 per cent) of the time that younger people spend on the Internet on a computer is spent communicating with other people, comprised of 29 per cent social networking, 19 per cent email and 19 per cent instant messaging.

20 per cent of 16-24s have accessed the Internet through a games console and just a quarter of the time they spend on their mobiles is on voice calls.

There is also a growing use of technology among older people, although they typically focus on a narrower range of services.

In 2009, growth in Internet take-up appears to have been driven by older age groups. For the first time, half (50 per cent) of over-55s have broadband at home and they consider emails to be the most important media activity, with 36 per cent of over-55s using email each day and 47 per cent using email at least once a week.

Social networking grows across all age groups

Younger people are more likely to access social networking sites, with 61 per cent of 15-34s claiming to do so, compared to 40 per cent of all adults – up ten per cent on 2008.

But it is by no means exclusively a young person's activity.

Nearly half of 35-54s claim to use social networking sites, as do 20 per cent of 55-64s – the latter showing a seven per cent increase over the past year.

Social networking accounts for nearly a quarter of all time spent on the Internet (23 per cent compared to nine per cent in 2007).

This has been driven by the rapid growth of Facebook – which is up 31 per cent – and the average Facebook user spent six hours and 30 minutes on the site during May 2010.

Facebook was also the most popular mobile Internet site in terms of time spent, accounting for almost half (45 per cent) of total time spent online on mobiles in December 2009.

Men, women and their media

Men spend nearly an hour more per day using media than women – an average of seven hours 33 minutes per day compared with six hours 38 minutes.

Men (25 per cent) are also more likely than women (21 per cent) to use their phones to access the Internet, although over the past year the gap between the proportions of men and women who use their mobiles for web access has halved from eight percentage points to four percentage points.

Women use their phones more in their own time than at work (71 per cent landline calls, 85 per cent mobile calls), compared to men (54 per cent landline calls, 63 per cent mobile calls).

Women said that they would miss their mobile phone (15 per cent) and landline (eight per cent) more than men (12 per cent mobile phones, two per cent landlines) and, while women rate social networking on a computer as a more important activity to them than men, they spend about the same amount of time doing it daily (18 minutes compared with 20 minutes).

Usage up, spending down

Households are consuming more communications and media – more voice calls, more texts, more data and more TV viewing.

But communications spend now accounts for a lower proportion of total household expenditure (4.4 per cent in 2009 compared to 4.6 per cent in 2008) and overall household spend on telecoms services has fallen by over 17 per cent in real terms in the last five years.

The trend to buy communications services in bundles has also grown significantly over the past five years.

Rise in 'bundled' communications services

Half of all UK households now buy two or more services from a single provider compared to 29 per cent in 2005. 70 per cent of people with a bundle said that the main reason for taking one was because it was cheaper.

The recession also led to a change in consumer opinion about the deals operators offer. 88 per cent of consumers believed that at least one operator was offering better deals than they were 12 months ago. Only 13 per cent thought that no providers were offering better deals compared to 25 per cent a year ago.

Consumers are also now more likely to use online shopping to search for better deals.

Just over half (53 per cent) of respondents with broadband access agreed they were more likely to use the Internet to shop, while 61 per cent say they now use price comparison websites more frequently.

⇨ The above information is reprinted with kind permission from Ofcom. Visit http://consumers.ofcom.org.uk for more information.

© Ofcom

UK consumers revealed as early adopters of new technologies

UK consumers are some of the earliest adopters of new communications technologies, new Ofcom research reveals.

They are among the best connected for broadband, mobile and digital TV and the UK has seen the fastest growth in smartphone take-up. UK consumers are also enjoying lower prices for communications services than many consumers across the world.

Ofcom's fifth International Communications Market report into the global communications market looks at take-up, availability and use of broadband, landlines, mobiles, TV and radio in 17 countries.

UK households among the best connected

Take-up of communications services across the world is continuing at a rapid pace, despite the global recession. Ofcom's consumer research reveals that across the six countries it surveyed, expenditure on communications services remains resilient with people less likely to cut down on communications services, and in particular broadband (six-seven per cent), than they are on other areas such as nights out (39-56 per cent) or holidays (29-51 per cent).

UK households have comparatively high levels of take-up of communications services, with among the highest take-up of landlines, fixed broadband connections, mobile connections and digital TV at the end of 2009.

Germany has the highest landline take-up with 85 per cent of the population having a landline (84 per cent in the UK). Italy has the highest mobile take-up with 95 per cent of the population owning a mobile phone (91 per cent in the UK), and the Netherlands has the highest fixed broadband take-up (85 connections per 100 households, 70 in UK).

However, the UK is behind other countries in take-up of Voice over Internet Protocol (VoIP) services with only five subscribers for every 100 people, compared with 26 in France and 20 in the Netherlands, although the UK did see an average 27 per cent annual increase in

VoIP subscribers between 2006 and 2009. VoIP services tend to be more popular in countries where there is high demand for international calls or where broadband is available to consumers without the need for landline services (also known as Naked Digital Subscriber Line).

UK consumers prefer portable devices to use the Internet

Across most countries, the desktop PC is still the most popular device used to access the Internet at home, followed by the laptop. But in the UK the opposite is true, with laptops being the most popular device used to access the Internet at home, used by 69 per cent of Internet users. The UK is the only country surveyed where more than half of 18-24s (60 per cent) use a device other than a desktop PC to use the Internet.

Mobile Internet is also popular with people in the UK, with 29 per cent of Internet users saying they use their mobile to access the Internet at home, second only to those in Japan at 43 per cent. 14 per cent of UK and US consumers also use their games consoles to access the Internet, compared with seven per cent of Internet users in Germany.

UK sees fastest growth in smartphone take-up

The UK saw the highest growth in smartphone take-up in the past year, with a 70 per cent rise in subscriber numbers between January 2009 and January 2010, compared to 11 per cent in Italy. Italy has the highest take-up of smartphones overall among the comparator European countries, with 26 subscribers for every 100 people, followed by Spain (21) and the UK (18).

Spain, closely followed by the UK, also has the highest proportion of subscribers paying over £35 or €50 per month for their smartphone services (seven and six subscribers for every 100 people, respectively). High-value subscribers are more likely to use premium

handsets such as the iPhone. They are also more likely to have more bundled minutes and data, suggesting that subscribers plan to use their phones more often and for more functions. The UK experienced significantly faster growth in high-value subscribers than any other European country with 61 per cent growth, compared to Spain with just four per cent growth.

While downloading mobile apps varies little across comparator countries, use of mobile mapping and direction services has grown fastest in the UK (86 per cent increase since 2009), with nine in every 100 people in the UK using these services, compared to five in every 100 people in France and Germany.

UK consumers more likely to use mobiles for social networking

People in the UK are using their mobile phones for social networking more than in other countries, with 24 per cent of UK consumers compared to 13 per cent of people in Germany. Younger people in the UK are more likely to visit social networking sites on their mobiles than in other countries, with 45 per cent of 18-24s and 38 per cent of 25-34s saying that they did this.

The UK and Spain lead the way with digital TV take-up at 91 per cent

The number of social networkers is also higher in the UK than other comparator countries among 18-24s and 55-64s. 86 per cent of 18-24s in the UK say they use the Internet for social networking, compared to 77 per cent in France and 48 per cent in Japan.

45 per cent of 55-64s in the UK say they use the Internet for social networking compared to 30 per cent in Germany and 13 per cent in Japan. Overall, Italy has the highest percentage of adults who use the Internet for social networking at 63.4 per cent, closely followed by the UK and USA at 63.2 per cent.

Mobile messaging also continues to grow across the globe, with Australia having the highest average use at 254 text and picture messages per person per month. The UK is the second biggest text messaging nation in Europe after Ireland, with 140 messages per person per month (218 per person per month in Ireland).

UK leading the way in new TV technologies

The UK and Spain lead the way with digital TV take-up at 91 per cent, as digital switchover is implemented across the globe.

While UK consumers are ahead of the rest of the world in take-up of HD-ready TV sets (59 per cent of

UK households, ahead of the USA with 57 per cent), take-up of HDTV services is lower in the UK than in other countries, where take-up tends to be linked to the amount of HDTV channels available.

In the USA, 44 per cent of households have HDTV services with access to 404 HD channels, followed by Japan (43 per cent of households and 130 channels), France (42 per cent and 55 channels) and then the UK (13 per cent and 50 channels).

Overall, UK TV viewers watched more TV than the average 207 minutes per day, watching 225 minutes, unchanged from 2008. US TV viewers watched more TV than in any other country with 280 minutes per day, followed by Polish TV viewers with 240 minutes and Italians with 238 minutes.

The UK had the second highest number of homes with pay TV DVRs (such as Sky+ and V+) at the end of 2009 with 7.8 million devices, up by 40 per cent on 2008. The USA had the highest number of homes with DVR subscriptions with 34.7 million at the end of 2009, up by more than a quarter (26 per cent) year on year.

Ofcom's consumer research also found that the UK has more consumers watching TV on the Internet, with just under a quarter (24 per cent) of consumers claiming to do this every week. This rose to 45 per cent when asked whether they had ever accessed TV content on the Internet. People in the USA were the second most likely to watch TV on the Internet, with a fifth (22 per cent) using the Internet to watch TV on a weekly basis.

But UK behind on local TV services

The availability of local and regional TV services varies widely across the world and apart from Ireland (with six), the UK, with nine, has the fewest amount of local and regional TV services available compared to other European countries and the USA. By comparison, Italy has an estimated 631 and the USA has 4,758 local terrestrial TV services. The UK Government has identified this area as a development priority.

Lower prices in the UK for most communications services

Overall, prices for communications services in the UK compare favourably to those in the comparator countries – France, Italy, Germany, Spain, USA. In all of the European countries analysed, consumers can make significant savings by purchasing 'double-play' or 'triple-play' services rather than subscribing to the lowest price standalone services. The UK is cheaper for four out of the five baskets (landline phone, mobile phone, broadband) Ofcom compared, but once pay TV is also included, pricing in the UK is comparatively more expensive.

For example, for a basket typical of a family household with four mobile connections of varying use, broadband, landline and a basic pay-TV service, the research finds that the lowest service prices overall were available in the UK (£93 a month), followed by France (£106 a month). The lowest price for the landline, broadband and TV components is achieved by purchasing a triple-play service in the UK, France, Germany and Spain; however, the cost of this triple-play service is higher in the UK (£37 a month) than in Germany (£32), Spain (£28) and France (£26).

Much of the difference in prices is due to lower mobile prices in the UK, although the gap in mobile prices is narrowing as prices fell by ten per cent in the UK between July 2009 and July 2010, compared to a 25 per cent fall in Italy and a 23 per cent fall in Spain. Fixed-line prices are also lower in the UK but increased over the same period whereas they fell in other countries.

UK consumers spend more online

The research shows that Internet users in the UK say they made more than double the number of online purchases in the past six months than Internet users in any other major European country except Poland (19 and 14 online purchases, respectively). The next country was Germany with nine purchases.

In addition, the total value of online purchases Internet users said they made in the past six months was highest in the UK with £1,031. This was nearly double the amount spent by Internet users in the next-placed country, Germany, with £595.

Super-fast broadband around the corner

Despite super-fast broadband being available in some parts of the comparator countries, fewer than one in 50 households in the UK, France, Italy, Germany and Spain had a superfast broadband connection at the end of 2009. This compares to 34 per cent of Japanese households. However, around the world there are large scale deployments of superfast networks and the UK compares well with its target of 66 per cent of households to have access to next-generation broadband by 2015.

Mobile broadband speeds have also increased among the comparator countries with HSPA+ and LTE services technologies being deployed in most countries throughout 2009 and 2010, with maximum theoretical download speeds of 100 MBit/s now available in Sweden. However, consumers in the UK and France can only achieve maximum theoretical download speeds of 7.2 MBit/s via HSPA networks as they are yet to deploy these new technologies. UK mobile operators have set out plans to build and introduce LTE networks and services over the next few years.

Avid audio fans

Digital radio take-up in the UK was the highest among the countries Ofcom surveyed with almost a third (31 per cent) claiming to own and use a digital radio. Take-up was lowest in Japan (three per cent) and the USA (seven per cent).

Ownership and use of personal media players (such as MP3/MP4 and iPods) was highest in Italy, with nearly two-thirds (64 per cent) of people and was also high in the UK with just over half (52 per cent) of people claiming to own and use such a device.

High Internet and mobile advertising spend in UK

Overall, global communications revenues grew by just 0.3 per cent over the previous year, but global advertising expenditure fell by 13 per cent to £254 billion in 2009. TV remained the largest single source of advertising spend (38 per cent of total, a decline of nine per cent on the previous year) and Internet advertising expenditure grew one per cent between 2008 and 2009 to £37 billion. The Internet accounted for a larger proportion of advertising spend (27 per cent) in the UK than in any other comparator country.

Mobile advertising spend per capita in Japan outstrips its nearest rival, the UK, by a ratio of almost five to one – but the UK is growing rapidly in line with the increase in smartphone take-up. Advertisers in Japan spends £5.57 per capita, in the UK the figure is £1.14.

However, while TV and radio advertising has declined, TV and radio subscriptions have increased, despite the economic downturn. Pay TV subscriptions increased by 5.8 per cent, and satellite radio subscriptions grew by 5.1 per cent.

Telecoms revenues also declined in seven of the 17 comparator countries, up from three in 2008. Mobile revenues are not keeping pace with increases in take-up and use, with mobile connections increasing by 16.3 per cent and call volumes increasing by 14.7 per cent, but revenues increased by just 2.7 per cent. In broadband, the UK was unique as the only country where fixed broadband revenues fell in 2009, as a result of increased take-up of lower-cost LLU-based broadband services as part of double- and triple-play bundles.

2 December 2010

⇨ The above information is reprinted with kind permission from Ofcom. Visit www.ofcom.org.uk for more information.

© Ofcom

OFCOM

State of the blogosphere 2010

Information from Technorati.

Welcome to Technorati's *State of the Blogosphere 2010* report. Since 2004, our annual study has followed growth and trends in the blogosphere. For 2010, we took a deeper dive into the entire blogosphere, with a focus on female bloggers. This year's topics include: brands embracing social media; traditional media vs. social media; brands working with bloggers; monetisation; smartphone and tablet usage; importance of Twitter and Facebook; niche blogging, and changes within the blogosphere over 2010.

Summary of key findings

The 2010 edition of *State of the Blogosphere* finds blogs in transition – no longer an upstart community, now with influence on mainstream narratives firmly entrenched, with bloggers still searching for the next steps forward. Bloggers' use of and engagement with various social media tools is expanding, and the lines between blogs, micro-blogs and social networks are disappearing. As the blogosphere converges with social media, sharing of blog posts is increasingly done through social networks – even while blogs remain significantly more influential on blog content than social networks are.

The significant growth of mobile blogging is a key trend this year. Though the smartphone and tablet markets are still relatively new and most analysts expect them to grow much larger, 25% of all bloggers are already engaged in mobile blogging. And 40% of bloggers who report blogging from their smartphone or tablet say that it has changed the way they blog, encouraging shorter and more spontaneous posts.

> **40% of bloggers who report blogging from their smartphone or tablet say that it has changed the way they blog**

Another important trend is the influence of women and mum bloggers on the blogosphere, mainstream media and brands. Their impact is perhaps felt most strongly by brands, as the women and mum blogger segment is the most likely of all to blog about brands. In addition to conducting our blogger survey, we interviewed 15 of the most influential women in social media and the blogosphere.

These changes are occurring in the context of great optimism about the medium: over half of respondents plan on blogging more frequently in the future, and 43% plan on expanding the topics that they blog about. Bloggers who get revenue from blogging are generally blogging more this year than they were last year. And 48% of all bloggers believe that more people will be getting their news and entertainment from blogs in the next five years than from the traditional media. We've also asked consumers about their trust and attitudes toward blogs and other media: 40% agree with bloggers' views, and their trust in mainstream media is dropping.

⇨ The above information is reprinted with kind permission from Technorati.com. Visit www.technorati.com for more information.

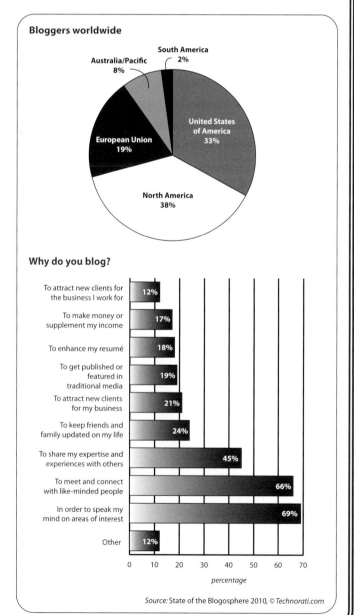

Bloggers worldwide

- South America 2%
- Australia/Pacific 8%
- United States of America 33%
- European Union 19%
- North America 38%

Why do you blog?

- To attract new clients for the business I work for — 12%
- To make money or supplement my income — 17%
- To enhance my resumé — 18%
- To get published or featured in traditional media — 19%
- To attract new clients for my business — 21%
- To keep friends and family updated on my life — 24%
- To share my expertise and experiences with others — 45%
- To meet and connect with like-minded people — 66%
- In order to speak my mind on areas of interest — 69%
- Other — 12%

percentage (0 10 20 30 40 50 60 70)

Source: State of the Blogosphere 2010, © Technorati.com

Reality TV and Facebook – the worst innovations of the last decade

Reality television, Facebook, Twitter and congestion charging are some of the worst innovations of the last decade, according to a survey which has highlighted the most beneficial and negative ideas to have changed our lives in recent years.

By Harry Wallop

The Internet dominates both the best and worst lists, with home broadband followed by online shopping the two ideas to have made the most positive contribution to our lives. Google, the search engine, comes in at third place.

A decade ago, just over a quarter of the population had the Internet at home, with nearly all of it via a slow dial-up connection, making booking a holiday, viewing pictures or buying an item of clothing a painfully slow business.

Last year 73 per cent of the population had the Internet at home, according to the Office for National Statistics, with most of those people enjoying a broadband connection.

A decade ago, just over a quarter of the population had the Internet at home... Last year 73 per cent of the population had the Internet at home

However, the Internet is also responsible for many ideas that people don't appreciate, including Twitter, the micro blogging site; Facebook, the social network; and Pop-up advertising, all of which make it into the top five innovations that have had the most negative effect on our lives.

The shortlist of the innovations of the decade was drawn up by The Foundation, a consultancy which advises retailers, banks and other consumer companies. The list was then voted on by 2,200 consumers.

Charlie Dawson, a partner at The Foundation, pointed out that the majority of the population now pay for broadband – something that was not even available more than a decade ago. He said: 'This survey is a reminder of how useful broadband has become for most people in the UK. It allows us to do lots of things more quickly, more effectively and with a lot less effort, from shopping to dating to finding stuff out.'

The roots of reality television stretch far back, but it took off in Britain in 2000 with *Castaway*, featuring Ben Fogle, now a presenter and *Telegraph* columnist, and others living on a remote Scottish Island for a year. It was swiftly followed by *Big Brother* and an increasing line of more downmarket and exploitative shows.

The main reason the format topped the list, along with Facebook and Twitter, was 'irritation' and 'time-wasting', according to those surveyed.

The roots of reality television stretch far back, but it took off in Britain in 2000 with Castaway, featuring Ben Fogle

Technology is also behind the fourth most-hated innovation: automated call centres, which force consumers – trying to ring up their utility company or bank – to listen to a machine telling them to push numbers on their telephone keypad.

Green measures feature on both the worst and best list, with community recycling schemes, such as Freecycle, being warmly welcomed as a way of obtaining cheap products and ensuring cast-offs go to a good home.

However, paying for plastic bags, an idea pioneered by Marks & Spencer, made the most-hated list. The idea was meant to save millions of bags ending up in landfill, but some shoppers now complain that they are left with a mountain of 'bags for life' cluttering up their kitchens.

The innovations of that have contributed the most to Britain in the last ten years

1 Home broadband

2 Online shopping

3 Google

4 Chip and Pin

5 Digital cameras/photography

6 Online comparison sites

7 Community recycling

8 Health labelling on foods (e.g. traffic lights)

9 Low-cost air travel

10 Consumer GPS/sat-nav

The innovations of that have contributed the least to Britain in the last ten years

1　Reality TV

2.　Facebook and similar

3　Pop-up advertising

4　Twitter

5　IVR/Interactive voice response on telephones

6　Congestion charging

7　Paid-for plastic bags

8　DVD membership schemes (e.g. Lovefilm)

9　Tracker mortgages

10　Public bike schemes

18 February 2011

Twitter adds 100 million new users in 2010

Microblogging service Twitter had 100 million new sign-ups this year, the site has revealed, including high-profile celebrity users such as Bill Gates, Tiger Woods and Kanye West.

By Claudine Beaumont

More than 100 million people joined microblogging service Twitter this year, the company has revealed.

Tiger Woods, Bill Gates, Kanye West and Cher have all signed up to the service in the last 12 months.

The site now has around 200 million users, and is widely recognised as a vital source of breaking news and views, providing real-time, eyewitness accounts of events such as the Iran election protests, the crash-landing of an aircraft on the Hudson River and the earthquake in Haiti.

According to new research from the Pew Internet & American Life Project, eight per cent of adult Internet users in America are on Twitter, with that figure rising to 14 per cent of 18- to 29-year-olds.

Almost a quarter of Twitter users check the service several times a day, although 21 per cent said they never checked it at all, suggesting that some people sign up to the service but don't use it.

The study also revealed that African-American and Latino adult Internet users in the United States were twice as likely as white American adults to use Twitter.

Around 13 per cent of Latino adult web users and 18 per cent of African-American adult web users also use Twitter, compared to just eight per cent of white adults.

Minority groups are bigger users of the micro-blogging service because they are younger and more connected to mobile technology, said the study.

'Both of those groups, African-American and Latino adult Internet users in the US, tend to be younger than white Internet users, which helps to lead to their adoption of Twitter,' said Aaron Smith, a senior research specialist with the Pew project.

'Both of those groups are also very mobile populations in their use of cell phones in particular to access the web. Overall, non-whites are more likely than white cell phone owners to do a range of non-voice tasks on their cell phones. They are more likely to use instant messaging and social networking on their phones.'

10 December 2010

THE TELEGRAPH

Websites and iPads – which way now for newspapers?

Some newspapers are closing their websites to everyone but paying customers; and then, there's the Apple iPad. What's the future for newspaper websites?

By James Cridland

An introduction to newspapers in the UK

Rupert Murdoch, the owner of (among others) *The Sun* and *The Times*, was clear in April 2010 on his thoughts about the future. 'We are going to stop people like Google or Microsoft or whoever from taking stories for nothing … there is a law of copyright and they recognise it,' he told an event in the US.

In June 2010, *The Times* and *The Sunday Times* became paid-for websites, behind a so-called 'paywall'. Murdoch's '*Wall Street Journal*' had already moved to a pay model some years earlier, in a move that earns the newspaper around $65 million a year; Murdoch's wish is to emulate this with all his titles around the world.

It's not going to be easy. While the *Wall Street Journal* contains specialist business news and analysis which is exclusive to the newspaper, *The Times* is a rather more general title, containing little which is specifically exclusive. In addition, the UK landscape is significantly altered by the presence of the BBC website, which is funded by the licence fee. Many media specialists claim that *The Times* will lose almost all of its online audience.

Further, Murdoch's claim, many argue, is based on a falsehood. Google News doesn't 'take stories for nothing': it retrieves a headline and an initial sentence from a news story, crediting the story and linking through to the original. Critics claim that Google News is actually good news for the newspapers, since it results in additional visitors. Other critics point to Google News's surprising unpopularity: it represents a fraction of Google's traffic (and doesn't appear to carry advertising). Others point to the fact that it's always been possible to remove your website from Google altogether: something that no Murdoch paper has done.

Some argue that this is a useful test of whether UK readers will pay for news; yet Johnston Press has already done such an experiment. It was quietly dropped after the number of people subscribing to some titles had been 'in single figures'.

Perhaps the newspaper industry's brighter hopes are with the iPad. The device is a thin tablet computer which, by itself, is not a particularly game-changing product: it joins similar products that Microsoft have been building since the early 2000s. However, Apple have complete control of the device's software, and a relationship with every customer. Users can purchase apps from the device (with all billing handled by Apple), and – crucially – users can purchase subscriptions to content within apps. Delivery of news content via an app on the iPad can be monetised without users needing to find their credit card or remember another username or password; and it's this that enables an opportunity for the newspaper and magazine industry.

The iPad is a new device, and time will tell whether it represents a new opportunity for the publishing industry. Since the iPad can also surf the web, one potential drawback for publishers is that their websites look simply too good, making an app unnecessary. Critics point to the control of Apple being a potential free-speech issue. However, it would be a foolish media commentator who simply ignores the part that the iPad could play in the future of printed media.

28 June 2010

⇨ The above information is reprinted with kind permission from Media UK. Visit www.mediauk.com for more information.

© *Media UK*

What is WikiLeaks?

It is the organisation behind the biggest leak of secret information since the Vietnam 'Pentagon Papers' were made public nearly 40 years ago. But what is WikiLeaks? Channel 4 News examines the whistleblowers' website.

WikiLeaks brings information to the public which its founders believe the public has a right to know.

Often, this information is exactly the kind which the organisations and governments involved would really much rather the public did not know.

Set up in Sweden in 2006 by Julian Assange, *Time Magazine* said it could have as much of an impact on journalism as the Freedom of Information Act.

What is WikiLeaks?

WikiLeaks is a website set up by a group of human rights activists, technical people and journalists to bring sensitive materials to the attention of the public.

In an exclusive interview with Channel 4 News, WikiLeaks founder Julian Assange described the service as: 'an international public service that helps whistleblowers or journalists get suppressed information out to the public – and do it safely'.

The team obtains, publishes and defends such materials, usually from anonymous sources, and also fights in the legal and political spheres for the broader principles on which it is based: 'the integrity of our common historical record and the rights of all peoples to create new history'.

Once a WikiLeaks document is published, the team will fight not to censor or remove the information through its team of lawyers. It also fights to protect its sources.

On its website, the team describe WikiLeaks as, in a sense, 'the first intelligence agency of the people'. Despite the name, its only real connection to Wikipedia is the name and presentation style. The public cannot edit anything on WikiLeaks, which is instead controlled by a small team of professionals.

It has a presence in a number of countries to benefit from different legal environments, but is believed to have originally been established in Sweden in 2006. It is banned by the Chinese government.

Why was it set up?

The founders say that they set up WikiLeaks to protect people who want to bring secrets out into the public domain, across the globe. Their aim is to make government activities more transparent, leading to less corruption, better governance and stronger democracies.

WikiLeaks says that obtaining this information has traditionally been costly, both in terms of human life and human rights. But technological advances mean that the risks of getting this kind of information out there are lower.

Who is behind WikiLeaks?

It is run by a company called the Sunshine Press. Its main spokesman, and founder, is an Australian called Julian Assange, who spoke to Channel 4 News about the site in a rare interview.

He said the site is different to others because of the way it works.

'The key difference is that we have a stated commitment to a particular kind of process and objective, and that commitment is to get censored material out and never to take it down,' he said.

'That commitment has driven our technical and legal process and has resulted in sources understanding that we are the most trusted organisation to give material to and we always fight attempted censorship and have always won. That kind of moral clarity of our position has got us a lot of support – from sources wanting to give us material and from journalists and free press advocates who know that we should be supported because we're the vanguard of an ideal which is that justice comes about as a result of the disclosure of abuse.'

CHANNEL 4

The site began as an online dialogue between activists in different parts of the globe, who were concerned that people were suffering as a result of resources being diverted through corruption of governance.

Who is Julian Assange?

The founder of WikiLeaks does not court publicity.

Once asked by a reporter for a face-to-face meeting, he apparently retorted: 'What'd you want to see – the way I move my eyebrows?'

He has never officially given his age, but is believed to be a 37-year-old Australian who set up WikiLeaks as part of a crusade to make governments accountable.

WikiLeaks is a website set up by a group of human rights activists, technical people and journalists to bring sensitive materials to the attention of the public

---

He's broken his silence for Channel 4 News, but it's no surprise he's keeping his head down: he's made quite a few enemies since setting up WikiLeaks in 2006, including, he says, the Pentagon.

He says WikiLeaks, which has more than a million documents online, has fought off more than 100 lawsuits – so he clearly does not shy away from a fight.

According to *The Times* newspaper, he was arrested as part of a group of computer hackers in 1989, when, just as the Atlantis space shuttle was about to be launched, NASA's computer monitors showed one giant word – 'Wank', the acronym for hacker group Worms Against Nuclear Killers. Assange was one of six Melbourne teens arrested by police. Although never implicated in the NASA attack, he was charged with more than 30 counts of computer crime, placed on a 'good behaviour bond' and fined about £1,275 in today's money.

Since 1989, it is believed he worked in computer security and raised a son. He also took a mathematics and physics course at Melbourne University.

He is believed to have lived in a number of countries around the world, and evaded capture from people who don't share his beliefs a number of times.

His inspiration for WikiLeaks is said to have come from one of the most notorious leaks of all time: when in 1971 top-secret papers about America's political and military involvement in Vietnam were brought to light in the *New York Times*, which became known as the 'Pentagon Papers'.

As an organisation, WikiLeaks remains quite secretive as a result of the nature of the information it works with, and to avoid detection. It only employs a small number of staff, and is funded through a mixture of small donations and other funders with deeper pockets.

What has it done?

WikiLeaks has published secret information obtained from sources across the world.

Two of its biggest leaks, which made headlines globally, were in Kenya and Iraq.

In Kenya, before the 2007 election, WikiLeaks exposed $3,000,000,000 of Kenyan corruption, which they say swung the vote by ten per cent and led to enormous changes in the Kenyan constitution as well as the establishment of a more open government.

From Iraq, WikiLeaks uncovered a video of a helicopter attack by the US military in which a number of people died, including two Reuters journalists.

The black-and-white video shows US Apache helicopters in a Baghdad suburb, opening fire on a group of men, including two men identified by WikiLeaks as Reuters photographer Namir Noor-Eldeen and driver Saeed Chmagh.

The helicopter then fires on a van as those on board try to flee. The video also shows ground troops carrying two injured children from the van.

The incident took place in 2007, and Reuters spent several years attempting to get the US authorities to investigate or release the video before it appeared on WikiLeaks titled 'Collateral Murder'.

Who are the whistleblowers?

It is a key question – and no doubt on the lips of the US authorities over the latest leak.

But WikiLeaks' founder Julian Assange told Channel 4 News that, often, their security is so tight, they themselves do not even know, and he said that was the case in this leak.

'So other journalists try to verify sources,' he said. 'We don't do that, we verify documents. We don't care where it came from, but we can guess that it probably came from somewhere in the US military or the US government, from someone who is disaffected. Clearly a heroic act by the whistleblower. The system we have deployed to make whistleblowers to us untraceable also prevents us knowing who they are.'

However, occasionally whistleblowers do confess, or are exposed.

A US military analyst called Bradley Manning is currently

in detention in Kuwait, charged with leaking the video of a US helicopter attack in Iraq in which, WikiLeaks suggests, 12 people died, including two Reuters journalists.

WikiLeaks has never said whether he is the source, but is understood to have hired lawyers to work on his case.

Manning, 22, was arrested after boasting to a high-profile former hacker, Adrian Lamo, that he passed the material to WikiLeaks. He also said at the time that he passed thousands of pages of confidential American diplomatic cables to WikiLeaks as well.

Lamo said he was concerned by Manning's claim that he had sent 260,000 pages of cables to WikiLeaks.

'Hilary Clinton, and several thousand diplomats around the world, are going to have a heart attack when they wake up one morning, and find an entire repository of classified foreign policy is available, in searchable format, to the public,' Manning is said to have written.

It has not been proven whether Manning sent the cables or whether they are in any way connected to the leaks on Afghanistan.

Assange declined to comment to Channel 4 News on the source for the information, saying it was technologically impossible to say who the source was. At other points, he has also said that WikiLeaks did not have the cables Manning claimed to have sent.

Does it verify its documents, or its sources?

Not in the same way other media organisations would, but it does work hard to ensure its documents are real.

Rather than proving the source – indeed, WikiLeaks sometimes does not know its source for reasons of security – it instead goes to the area the document covers to try and verify the document itself.

It also has a team checking whether the document is a forgery. The team says that, to date, it has not published any fake documents.

Often it receives encrypted information, and has to break the code. It gets information from all kinds of areas – from postal drops to face-to-face meetings.

WikiLeaks' staff write the document summaries, and they cannot be edited.

Has anyone tried to stop it?

Yes – and sometimes they have, albeit briefly, succeeded. For example, in 2008 Swiss bank Julius Baer got a court ruling to take the main site off the web after WikiLeaks printed documents relating to its offshore activities. However, other versions remained online, and after international pressure from media and civil liberties groups, the bank dropped the case and the main site remained online as well.

WikiLeaks also has a very sophisticated hosting platform, thanks in no small part to founder Julian Assange's experience in computing. It also has robust defences which ensure the site cannot be hacked.

However, it has struggled with funding, and last year was temporarily shut down, before re-appearing in 2010.

How far will WikiLeaks go?

Too far, according to some commentators, who fear that public safety could be sacrificed in the rush for information.

But, as Assange told Channel 4 News, the website operates a 'harm minimisation process' which means that it would not publish information it believed would cause more harm than good.

> ## Wikileaks also has a very sophisticated hosting platform... [and] ...has robust defences which ensure the site cannot be hacked

He said: 'Sources know when they submit material that we go through a harm minimisation process. That harm minimisation process is not about removing material, it's about minimising harm. We have a number of ways to do that.

'The way we have done it in the past and it's always been effective – notify and delay. Notify the people concerned and delay the publication as a result.'

When asked if this harm minimisation process meant he would publish highly sensitive information such as weapon locations, CIA reports and even nuclear launch codes, he responded: 'After they've been changed – the launch codes – then we could publish it. That would reveal that the process of securing these things are a big problem and, as we all should know, nuclear war while quite distant, is still technically possible.'

25 July 2010

⇨ The above information is reprinted with kind permission from Channel 4. Visit their website at www.channel4.com for more information on this and other related topics.

Traditional papers didn't know how to handle WikiLeaks

WikiLeaks' revelations were fascinating – but the key points were too often overlooked by the press, writes Arianna Huffington.

With condolences to the iPad and Sarah Palin's Twitter account, WikiLeaks is the media story of our time. Since the one-two punch of the release of military reports about the wars in Iraq and Afghanistan, and November's trove of diplomatic cables, the Government, the media and the public have been playing catch-up with the implications of this new media frontier.

Much of the traditional media has seemed lost on how to handle this hi-tech interloper. As a result, too much of the coverage has been meta – focusing on questions about whether the leaks were justified – while too little has dealt with the details of what has actually been revealed and what those revelations say about the wisdom of America's ongoing effort in Afghanistan. There's a reason why the Obama administration has been so upset about these leaks.

As has too often been the case since 9/11, the WikiLeaks controversy has found a great deal of the media once again on the wrong side of the secrecy debate. As Harvard's John Perry Barlow tweeted: 'We have reached a point in our history where lies are protected speech and the truth is criminal.'

Whether old or new, the media's job, as Simon Jenkins wrote in the *Guardian*, isn't to protect the powerful from embarrassment. Its job is to play the role of the little boy in *The Emperor's New Clothes* – brave enough to point out what nobody else will say. And when the press trades truth for access, it is WikiLeaks that acts like the little boy.

Without that little boy, we get truth-for-access traders like Judith Miller, whose breathless, spoon-fed – and ultimately inaccurate – accounts from Iraq helped lead America to war. When her facts proved wrong, Miller shrugged it off by saying: 'My job isn't to assess the Government's information and be an independent intelligence analyst myself. My job is to tell readers of the *New York Times* what the Government thought about Iraq's arsenal.' In other words, her job is to tell citizens what their government is saying, not what their government is doing.

The establishment media may be part of the media, but they're also part of the establishment. And, with WikiLeaks, they've been circling the wagons. They conflate the secrecy that governments use to operate and the secrecy that allows governments to mislead us. Nobody, including WikiLeaks, is promoting the idea that governments should exist in total transparency, or that, for instance, all government meetings should be live-streamed and cameras placed around the White House like a DC-based spin-off of *Big Brother*.

But a government's legitimate need for secrecy is different from the government's desire to get away with hiding the truth. Conflating the two is dangerously unhealthy for a democracy. This is why it's especially important to look at what WikiLeaks is doing, as distinct from what its critics claim it's doing.

The public have been playing catch-up with the implications of this new media

It's also important to look at the fact that even though the cables were published in mainstream outlets such as the *Guardian*, the information first went to WikiLeaks. 'You've heard of voting with your feet?' said New York University journalism professor Jay Rosen. 'The sources are voting with their leaks. If they trusted the newspapers more, they would be going to the newspapers.'

And what of the WikiLeaks themselves? Instead of one smoking-gun, bombshell revelation, the leaks have added to a consistent drip of damning and embarrassing details about the Afghanistan war and the brass tacks of diplomacy. For one thing, it turns out that the world of diplomats and ambassadors, which we always supposed to be a realm of intrigue, is kind of like high school. So it has been drip, drip, drip and the effect has been cumulative – not unlike mercury poisoning.

If any of the WikiLeaks revelations remind us why bringing allied troops home from Afghanistan quickly needs to be more – much more – than 'aspirational' (as the Pentagon recently termed the goal of being out by 2014), then the advent of the WikiLeaks era, and its implications for the wider media, will be a very good thing indeed.

This is about our future. For our democracies to survive, citizens have to be able to know what their government is really doing. We can't change course if we don't have accurate information about where we really are. Whether this comes from a new media website or an old media newspaper – or both – doesn't matter a lick.

5 February 2011

THE GUARDIAN

Freedom of information in the WikiLeaks era

'Is the whistleblowing site doing more harm than good?'
asks panel. Report by Judith Townend for Inforrm's Blog.

Julian Assange is more than capable of dominating a room he's not actually in, showed Monday's event at the British Institute of International and Comparative Law, 'Freedom of Information in the WikiLeaks Era'.

His lawyer Mark Stephens, however, was there to articulate (if not represent) WikiLeaks' and Assange's position and activity as he understood it.

A panel, chaired by legal commentator Joshua Rozenberg and also including David Banisar (Article 19), Chris Bradshaw (Ministry of Justice), Andrew Murray (LSE), and James Leaton Gray (BBC) alongside Stephens, discussed the ethics, role and legal implications of WikiLeaks and similar operations.

WikiLeaks good or WikiLeaks bad, Rozenberg asked at the end. Stephens had already left the room by that point, but the audience could probably could guess his answer.

'Both,' said Article 19's senior legal counsel David Banisar. Bad, in the context of the UK, said the MoJ's Bradshaw. 'Bad,' said Murray. 'Inevitable,' said the BBC's Leaton Gray.

But prior to that question, the WikiLeaks issue was fleshed out by the panellists with several key questions emerging:

⇨ Can the Freedom of Information (FoI) Act prevent the need for leaks? Where are its limitations?

⇨ Who is a journalist? What is a journalistic operation?

One successful outcome has been WikiLeaks' influence on media method, said Banisar

---

⇨ How to make the balance between right to freedom of expression and right to privacy?

⇨ How should/could WikiLeaks be regulated?

⇨ How can WikiLeaks' material be verified?

⇨ Is WikiLeaks a 'source' or a commercial partner to the media organisations it works with?

⇨ Do public bodies have a right to keep parts of the decision-making process private?

⇨ Do states have a right to privacy?

⇨ What are the legal issues arising from the emergence of 'citizen' journalism?

Article 19's David Banisar put WikiLeaks into context: while it had 'garnered the public imagination' and done things differently, the organisation was not the first online whistleblower, and he cited Cryptome as an early example. 'If you were in the techie world, you knew about Cryptome.' Additionally, the 'end of government as we know it' had been slightly exaggerated, he said.

Banisar, who worked for Privacy International before joining Article 19, said that WikiLeaks came under a media umbrella, but also acted as an intermediary between people with information, and the media.

One successful outcome has been WikiLeaks' influence on media method, said Banisar; Al Jazeera's Palestine Papers have provided actual documents, as opposed to analysis of the documents. That's a 'step forward', he said, and gives 'context and understanding'.

Chris Bradshaw, a lawyer in the Information and Human Rights team in Legal Directorate of the Ministry of Justice, argued that leaks are generally harmful and government

JUDITH TOWNEND

information should be accessed through Freedom of Information mechanisms.

He set out the Freedom of Information process, stating that FoI officers have a duty to advise and assist people who make requests. The audience were treated to some stats: of 17,822 requests in 2009, 59% had been disclosed in full, and 29% withheld in full. The most common reason for withholding data was its personal nature.

Ministers and officials need to be able to discuss issues in private, with 'thinking space', he said. There is an effective route for disclosure through FoI, and large-scale unauthorised leaks risk adverse effects, he concluded.

Andrew Murray, Reader in Law at the London School of Economics pursued a rather more academic line, examining WikiLeaks' social basis and which legal and moral norms apply.

Referring to the central tension between right to freedom of expression and right to privacy, he said that social norms play a role in how material is treated by the media. Media illegally obtained via phone hacking is rightfully vilified, whereas material such as Bradley Manning's alleged leak is repeated in newspapers.

Media illegally obtained via phone hacking is rightfully vilified, whereas material such as Bradley Manning's alleged leak, is repeated in newspapers

---

Murray also touched on the advent of digital publishing, where anyone can be a journalist but do not necessarily want to obey journalists' publishing rules.

In recent times, the government has employed more and more communication directors, he said, with spin as the 'natural response' to attempts to invade government privacy.

Former journalist James Leaton Gray may work at a media organisation, but he had his gamekeeper hat on for last night's debate, as head of the BBC's Information Policy and Compliance department.

In terms of his organisation's duty under FoI, he thought it was the right of the BBC and other public broadcasters to have a private space to consider significant editorial matters.

Reminding us that *Hansard* began as illegal scribblings in the Gallery, he said that WikiLeaks was another test of the freedom of expression balance.

While digital technology had improved accessibility and speed for releasing information, it was a retrograde step for providing context, he argued.

'I still want a journalist to act as a filter for me,' he said – not least because he didn't want to sift through 250,000 documents online.

So, to Julian Assange's lawyer, Mark Stephens, left to present WikiLeaks' approach. WikiLeaks is more responsible than anyone really wants to recognise, he said (answering a later question, he reported that Assange had refused an offer of a couple of million pounds for the cables – from someone in the Middle East).

In his talk, Stephens pointed out that the US Embassy cables had been available to three million people before the wider electorate were given access. Assange ran all the cables past the D-Notice committee and the Americans, he said.

'They were offered the opportunity to identify any single cable,' he said, which would fail the test of 'we will not endanger life or an ongoing operation'. 'That's the touchstone test that the D-Notice committee has.'

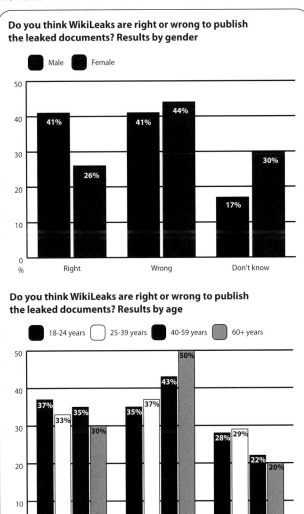

Do you think WikiLeaks are right or wrong to publish the leaked documents? Results by gender

Do you think WikiLeaks are right or wrong to publish the leaked documents? Results by age

Sample size: 2099 GB adults. Fieldwork: 18-19 October 2010. Source: YouGov (www.yougov.com)

JUDITH TOWNEND

All of the cables passed that test, he claimed: 'There were some exceptions and they were taken out and not used.' One story which the Americans didn't want published concerned bombing in Yemen. This caused a big discussion between the media partners [the *Guardian*, the *New York Times*, *Der Spiegel*, *Le Monde* and *El País*], he said, but in the end they decided it was of such importance to the public that they should publish.

Freedom of Information officers have a duty to advise and assist people who make requests. Of 17,822 requests in 2009, 59% had been disclosed in full, and 29% withheld in full

---

'No harm came as a consequence of that but one could see the point the Americans were making. There was a dialogue going on.'

The whole process, Stephens argued, had been 'sensitive' and 'sensible'. 'Julian wanted to take longer over the redactions process than the *Guardian* did.'

Stephens raised a very interesting issue [and pertinent given news of Assange's new relationship with *The Telegraph*] – that of media exclusivity.

'What's interesting, you have on one side of the fence a journalist who really wants the scoop, they want the exclusive. Now that doesn't necessarily fit with someone who wants, on the other hand, freedom of information, or indeed, data in the public domain.

Assange wanted more media partners, he said. 'There were a number of journalists who felt they had a sort of given right to an exclusive relationship with Julian.'

'I understand they do feel very proprietorial about their relationships, but for Julian it's about spreading the data, spreading the information, and that is a difference.'

Stephens, echoing Banisar's earlier point, questioned whether leaking culture was so terribly different from how it was before. Newspapers have always offered the opportunity for people to deliver brown paper envelopes; now it's no longer just dog-eared photocopies, but discs full of data, he said.

One thing was clear: it was the anonymous electronic drop box that made WikiLeaks different. And it looks like it's a technique that could be here to stay – none of the panellists suggested otherwise.

Newspapers have always offered the opportunity for people to deliver brown paper envelopes; now it's no longer just dog-eared photocopies, but discs full of data, he said

---

As is usual, perhaps the point, at these type of events, more unanswered questions were raised and more difficult tensions identified: not just that of Article 8 vs Article 10, but between the varying motives of state/s, journalists, leakers – and their intermediaries.

2 February 2011

⇨ The above information is reprinted with kind permission from Judith Townend. Visit http://inforrm. wordpress.com for more information.

© Judith Townend

Regulation and self-regulation of the media

Information from In Brief.

Broadcast journalism

The Office of Communications (Ofcom) controls the statutory regulation of commercial television and radio stations in the UK. It is the regulating body which deals with who owns these organisations, how the programmes are transmitted and also programme content (including journalism).

Ofcom's powers include fining media organisations for breaching regulations and closing down illegal 'pirate' broadcasters (and even commercial broadcasters).

The Ofcom Broadcasting Code provides ethical rules which broadcast journalists must adhere to or face sanctions from their employers. The BBC is amongst those media organisations that are subject to Ofcom's regulations but its BBC Trust also sets out an ethical code for BBC journalists in their BBC Editorial Guidelines.

One crucial requirement of both Ofcom and the BBC's ethical code is that all broadcast journalists must produce politically impartial content although, of course, does not require them to be politically impartial themselves.

Such statutory regulation of broadcast journalism is in place due to what politicians have seen as its power to influence, offend or harm the public in some way. Important examples include distortion of the facts to manipulate the public's view of the news, encouraging any form of violence or tension and transmitting pornographic material to children (hence watersheds).

Print journalism

In terms of statutory regulation, there is no equivalent to Ofcom for print journalism. Therefore, except anti-monopoly legislation, they have been left to self-regulate and it is for this reason that they may express strong political views without sanction.

The Press Complaints Commission (PCC) is the self-regulatory body for the print journalism industry, created and funded by newspapers and magazines themselves. It does, however, retain some independence from the industry, which is necessary for obvious reasons. Its main role is to determine adjudications in the event of complaints about content in newspapers and magazines. The PCC also takes into consideration the activities of journalists as part of their information gathering.

The Editor's Code

The Press Complaints Commission Editors' Code of Practice, or PCC Code as it is incorrectly known, is the print journalist's guide to ethics. It is drawn up by a committee of editors and used by the PCC in their adjudications. The PCC does not have the power, like Ofcom, to shut down media organisations but it can force an editor to publish an adjudication against their newspaper or magazine promptly and with a PCC headline. The shame of such a situation for the editor and staff is thought by the PCC to be a powerful deterrent but this is the limit of the commission's powers. That said, a journalist who breaks the Editor's Code time and time again would be at risk of being fired from the newspaper or magazine.

The Editor's Code, as ratified on 1 August 2007, can be summarised as follows. The Code must be applied to both printed and online versions of publications. It is up to the editors and publishers to ensure that not only editorial staff but all external contributors to their publication (including non-journalists) observe the code.

Clause 1 on accuracy includes the statements:

⇨ The press must take care not to publish inaccurate, misleading or distorted information, including pictures.

⇨ A significant inaccuracy, misleading statement or distortion once recognised must be corrected, promptly and with due prominence, and – where appropriate – an apology published.

⇨ The press, whilst free to be partisan, must distinguish clearly between comment, conjecture and fact.

Clause 3 on privacy includes:

⇨ Everyone is entitled to respect for his or her private and family life, home, health and correspondence, including digital communications. Editors will be expected to justify intrusions into any individual's life without consent.

IN BRIEF

➪ It is unacceptable to photograph individuals in a private place without their consent. A private place can be public property where there is a reasonable expectation of privacy.

Clause 4 on harassment includes:

➪ Journalists must not engage in intimidation, harassment or persistent pursuit.

➪ They must not persist in questioning, telephoning, pursuing or photographing individuals once asked to desist; nor remain on their property when asked to leave and must not follow them.

➪ Editors must ensure these principles are observed by those working for them and take care not to use non-compliant material from other sources.

Clause 10 on clandestine devices and subterfuge includes:

➪ The press must not seek to obtain or publish material acquired by using hidden cameras or clandestine listening devices; or by intercepting private or mobile telephone calls, messages or emails; or by the

It is not limited to the above examples though; for instance, the code states that there is a public interest in freedom of expression itself. The PCC's job is to decide whether the public interest was served and the extent to which the material is in the public domain, or would become so. It is up to the editor/s in question to fully demonstrate evidence of these considerations if they invoke the public interest to explain their journalistic activities or content.

It is unacceptable to photograph individuals in a private place without their consent. A private place can be public property where there is a reasonable expectation of privacy

---

➪ The above information is reprinted with kind permission from In Brief. Visit www.inbrief.co.uk for more information.

© In Brief

One crucial requirement of both Ofcom and the BBC's ethical code is that all broadcast journalists must produce politically impartial content

---

unauthorised removal of documents or photographs; or by accessing digitally-held private information without consent.

➪ Engaging in misrepresentation or subterfuge, including by agents or intermediaries, can generally be justified only in the public interest and then only when the material cannot be obtained by other means.

Clause 14 states:

➪ Journalists have a moral obligation to protect confidential sources of information.

The public interest

The Editor's Code aims to protect the rights of the individual and the public's right to know. For this reason, many clauses (on Privacy, Harassment, Children, Children in sex cases, Hospitals, Reporting of crime, Clandestine devices and subterfuge and Payment to criminals) are covered by exceptions on public interest.

The public interest includes detecting or exposing crime or serious impropriety, protecting public health or safety and preventing the public from being misled by an action or statement of an individual or organisation.

IN BRIEF

Major reform of Press Complaints Commission proposed

The Media Standards Trust (MST) has today (Monday 25 January) submitted proposals to make the existing system of press self-regulation more effective, more accountable and more transparent while maintaining the key principles of self-regulation.

Can independent self-regulation keep standards high and preserve press freedom?, submitted today to the Press Complaints Commission's independent governance review, contains 28 recommendations for reform, supported by a survey commissioned specially for the submission and conducted by Ipsos MORI.

> *Just 5% of people think that an independent self-regulatory body should wait for a complaint from someone directly referred to in the article before investigating whether it is inaccurate*

The MST submission recognises the valuable mediation work done by the PCC, but shows that the public expect more. It then sets out how out how the PCC could be reformed to perform the wider self-regulatory role that the public now expects, without requiring any statutory backing.

According to the opinion survey conducted for the submission, the public prefers an independent self-regulatory body (52%) to a newspaper industry complaints body (8%) or a regulatory body set up by the government (17%).

Moreover, rather than the chief purpose of this body being to mediate complaints between a newspaper and complainant (which 12% expect), the public expects the main role of an independent self-regulator to be:

⇨ to monitor the press' compliance with a code of practice, on behalf of the public (48%)

⇨ to conduct investigations where there is significant public concern about wrongdoing (25%).

The public does not appear to support the PCC's current constitutional limitation of usually investigating only when a complaint is received from someone directly involved in the article. Just 5% of people think that an independent self-regulatory body should wait for a complaint from someone directly referred to in the article before investigating whether it is inaccurate.

Almost half (48%) believe that such a body should be obliged to investigate whether it is inaccurate.

The public also support greater transparency, for example that the press self-regulator:

⇨ makes the minutes of its meetings publicly available (79%); and

⇨ makes the identity of who is funding the regulator known (75%).

Martin Moore, director of the Media Standards Trust, said 'The Press Complaints Commission was established to act as a newspaper and magazine complaints mediation body. Since then public expectations, fuelled by the media, have changed.

'The public wants an independent self-regulator that, in addition to mediating complaints, monitors compliance with the code and conducts regular investigations. The PCC, as currently constituted, does not and cannot do this.

> *The public prefers an independent self-regulatory body (52%) to a newspaper industry complaints body (8%) or a regulatory body set up by the government (17%)*

'This submission outlines ways in which the current system can be reformed so that it can meet public expectations of independent self-regulation.'

This submission to the PCC's review of governance follows an earlier MST report, *A More Accountable Press: The Need for Reform*, which was published in February 2009.

25th January 2010

⇨ The above information is reprinted with kind permission from the Media Standards Trust. Visit www.mediastandardstrust.org for more information.

© Media Standards Trust

MEDIA STANDARDS TRUST

Security-related social networking issues abound in organisations

Information from Search Security.

By Ron Condon

Most security professionals are aware of the security-related social networking issues posed by popular sites such as Facebook, Twitter and MySpace. They may also know that criminals are increasingly focusing their efforts on social networking sites, where they hope to snare unsuspecting users, steal their personal details and infect their computers. But even security professionals may not realise the sheer scale of the social networking challenges.

Facebook Inc. now has more than 400 million active users globally

Facebook Inc. now has more than 400 million active users globally, a massive 229% increase from a year ago. The uptake of Twitter has been even sharper. Twitter Inc.'s co-founder Biz Stone recently trumpeted that the number of Twitter accounts had grown by 1,500% in a year; although he gave no absolute figures, it is clear the number of users is already in the tens, if not hundreds, of millions.

Whatever the precise numbers, the rise in social media usage during the last year has been dramatic, and users and social networking challenges are growing at a faster pace than most companies can manage.

A couple of recent reports from security vendors highlight the extent of social networking security issues, and many believe it is one that companies need to tackle sooner rather than later.

Security vendor Webroot Software Inc. recently released a report indicating that while users are increasingly aware of the danger of sharing too much information on social networking sites, most users are still wide open to attack.

The Boulder, Colorado-based vendor surveyed more than 1,100 users of Facebook, LinkedIn, MySpace, Twitter and some other social networks, and compared the findings with a similar study conducted a year ago.

On the plus side, 27% of users now block anyone finding their profile through a public search engine, up from 20% a year ago; 67% use different passwords for each of their social network accounts, up from 64% last year; and 47% know who can see their profile, up from 41%.

On the other hand, more than a quarter of survey respondents had never changed their default privacy settings, and more than three-quarters placed no restrictions on who could see their recent activity. Users between the ages of 18 and 29 were the most lax about protecting information, with 43% using the same password and 77% happy to click on any link sent by a friend.

Likewise, users are still willing to share personal information that could be of use to a criminal:

⇨ 61% of users displayed their birthdays;

⇨ 52% of users showed their places of birth;

⇨ 17% of users showed their mobile phone numbers.

At the same time, the amount of spam hitting social networking sites rose by 27% in the last year, according to Webroot, and much of it was used to try and lure recipients into clicking on infected websites or downloading malware.

'Our team has noted over 100 different variations of Koobface, a worm known to trick people into clicking links they shouldn't in order to infect their PCs and often convince them to provide credit card numbers to buy phony antivirus products, among other fraudulent activities,' said Jeff Horne, Webroot's director of threat research, in a statement.

SEARCH SECURITY

New research from Blue Coat Systems Inc. also noted a rapid rise in the use of social networking, which has triggered a change of tactics by criminals.

'Social networking was already gaining traction in 2008, but its popularity exploded in 2009,' the report said. 'Blue Coat Labs saw an increase of over 500% in the frequency with which people accessed social networking sites during 2009.'

The company said this trend has prompted criminals to exploit the poor security on these sites, with the top two web-based threats being fake antivirus software and fake video codecs (where users are invited to view a video, but need to download a codec, which turns out to be malware). As it points out, these attacks are unlike the drive-by attacks of recent years which exploited software vulnerabilities, and are designed just to exploit human trust.

Security-related social networking issues present corporate problems

But while lack of security is clearly a problem for individuals using social networking sites, it also can also have severe implications for employers. Individuals may share sensitive corporate information via Twitter or Facebook, and they make also pick up malware infections along the way.

Ever since the advent of social networking sites, companies have been divided over whether to allow their staff to indulge in social networking while at work. Opponents focused on the time-wasting aspects, and also on the network bandwidth consumed by users downloading and sharing YouTube videos. For example, a study last year by security service supplier Network Box Corp. revealed that 7.8% of corporate network bandwidth was consumed by YouTube and 4.4% by Facebook.

But attitudes are changing. Some companies are beginning to see social networking as a powerful new channel for marketing and communications with customers, and are embracing it with enthusiasm – despite any prevalent social networking challenges.

'There has to be a compromise – employees would not accept a ban,' said David Cowan, head of security for London-based consultants Plan-Net plc. 'But you have to realise that if you are opening up to social networking and other mobile devices, you are opening yourself up to greater concern and risk.'

According to Cowan, social networking is much harder to manage than other forms of communication, such as email. 'Unlike email, you can't put a disclaimer on the end of a social networking message,' he said. 'Someone could say something on a social networking site and attribute it to your company, and misrepresent you. With email, you have an email policy and you can enforce disclaimers, but here you have no control.'

Cowan said social networking security issues therefore must now be incorporated into enterprise information security policies and employees' acceptable usage guidelines. He commonly advises companies to provide as much help and advice as possible to ensure employees use social networking sites cautiously and abide by their organisations' social networking security policies.

'Social networking definitely needs to be integrated into the information security policy and user education,' Cowan said. 'You need to make it clear what you should do, and what you shouldn't do. And give examples to make the message clear.'

Nigel Hawthorn, head of European marketing for Blue Coat, agreed and mentioned that training needs to explain how easy it is to leak information. 'There is, for instance, a difference between Facebook and Twitter,' he said. 'With Facebook, you can limit your comments to just a few friends, whereas with Twitter, everyone can see it. Some people display astonishing naiveté on these sites.'

Hawthorn added that web URL filtering technology has a role to play in enforcing granular security policies. By categorising different webpages, companies can allow certain pages on Facebook, for example, while blocking others.

'It would also be a good idea to block executables from being downloaded from any social networking site, which I don't think many companies are doing,' Hawthorn added. 'That would stop malware such as Koobface from infecting machines.'

David Bennett, a business development manager with Webroot, said few companies include social networking security issues in their acceptable usage policies.

'This needs to happen so that people are educated when they join an organisation, and I'd also recommend a regular refresher, possibly on a quarterly basis, to ensure they remain aware of the policies,' Wood said. 'They also need to be educated, for example, about the need to change their account passwords on a regular basis.'

He also made the point that training and education need to be underpinned with technology that can protect remote and mobile users as well as those users on the corporate network: 'It's all about education, and backing that up with the right IT infrastructure.'

12 April 2010

⇨ The above information is reprinted with kind permission from Search Security. Visit www.searchsecurity.techtarget.co.uk for more information.

Reuters sets up social media guidelines

Reuters has published some social media guidelines in its handbook of journalism. Dean Wright, Reuters' global editor for ethics, innovation and news standards, announced the new guidelines yesterday.

While the guidelines encourage Reuters journalists to use social media and stress that it is a powerful new tool, Reuters journalists are asked to get in contact with their line manager if they want to use them in a professional context.

The guidelines also recommend journalists set up a professional account – alongside their private account. This advice is a rather stiff approach to social media, which is a world where professional and personal lives collide.

In general, the Reuters' social media guidelines stress the most important aspects of journalistic ethics is to always say you are a Reuters journalist, avoid being biased, be careful not to reveal your sources by publicly 'following' or becoming their 'friend', or not to tweet a scoop if Reuters wants to send it first over the wires.

the impact of re-publishing third-party material, BBC World Service director Peter Horrocks recently asked his staff to make better use of social media to take it more into account as a journalistic source. An approach that was answered by a mild uproar.

However, Wright agrees that journalists should have the ability 'to use their brains and to see – and report on – a world that's changing every day'. In his view, this demand of the profession also applies to social media usage.

11 March 2010

© Guardian News and Media Limited 2010

A lot of news organisations have found it hard to take a firm position on how their journalists should use social media

The social media guidelines are part of the news agency's advice about *Reporting from the Internet,* which cover general guidelines for their reporters' representation in online chat-rooms or online forums, or the use of online encyclopedias as a starting point for research, but not an attributable source.

Partly, Reuters' social media guidelines don't read like editorial guidelines, but like a useful instruction manual on how a journalist can get started in the new world of social media as they answer questions like 'What is Twitter?' and explain that social media feels private, but is public.

Reuters' struggle to encorporate social media with journalism is not an uncommon problem. A lot of news organisations have found it hard to take a firm position on how their journalists should use social media.

Shall journalists be incredibly wary when using social media? Or should they be expected to use it when it leads them to information?

While the BBC editorial guidelines mention social media only very briefly by warning its journalists to consider

Just what is privacy in the era of Google and Facebook?

Eight or so years ago, in one of those mad periods when MPs get all hot under the collar about intrusions into privacy, some think-tank or other decided to carry out research to discover what people considered to be private.

By Roy Greenslade

The results were far from straightforward. There were wide variations between what people believed should be private and what they thought could reasonably be made public.

But a single factor united almost all of them. The home represented true privacy. What went on behind closed doors in the privacy of their own home was sacrosanct.

It also became evident in that research, as it has in other studies before and since, that hypocrisy plays a large part in how people conceive privacy. They wish to know as much as possible about other people, especially the rich and famous, while being extremely protective of their own privacy.

That, of course, is one of the reasons for the success of popular newspapers and magazines down the ages, in Britain and the United States, and in countries across the world. Readers lap up the gossip and the innuendo.

It is a vicarious pleasure and the only 'victims' in most cases, though not all, are those who seek the limelight in order to feed their appetite for money or fame, or both.

That remains the case as far as mainstream media is concerned. Now, almost a decade on from the research I mentioned, the problem of maintaining one's privacy has widened to include the overwhelming majority of the population, meaning those who surf the Internet. Intrusion into privacy has assumed a wholly new dimension with the widespread use of the net.

The locked front doors of our homes are no longer an impenetrable barrier to outsiders. We sacrifice some of our claims to privacy the instant we purchase goods or services on the net, allowing cookies to be implanted on our computers. It mean that e-traders know more about our desires than we often know ourselves.

That is unconscious activity. Much more prevalent, and more worrying, is the phenomenon of social networking sites that encourage us to compromise our privacy by sharing our personal details, thoughts, pictures and videos with an expanding community of users.

In addition, there is Google. There is always Google, a search engine that is also a searcher. It restlessly seeks out new ways to expand its hugely successful brand into areas that also, at least potentially, intrude into privacy, not least through its controversial Street View feature.

It now transpires that aside from the initial concerns about Google's team of photographers picturing people engaging in activities that they would rather remain private, it also recorded communications sent from people's homes over unsecured wireless networks.

Intrusion into privacy has assumed a wholly new dimension with the widespread use of the net

Google has reluctantly admitted the transgression, after denying it initially, by explaining that it picked up the messages when its Street View vehicles started to assemble a database of electronic Wi-Fi addresses, in order, supposedly, to improve the functioning of its location services.

That could well lead to high-level investigations in Europe and the United States. As Peter Schaar, the German commissioner for data protection, noted, the 'accidental' collection of such material meant that 'the market leader on the Internet simply disobeyed normal rules'.

What, however, is normal nowadays when it comes to privacy? In a recent interview, Facebook's founder Mark Zuckerberg said he had taken an 'about face' on privacy and no longer believed it to be a 'social norm'.

I have watched that interview a couple of times to test whether he was being deliberately provocative by overstating his opinion. It appears not. He genuinely believes that within the lifetime of Facebook itself people have knowingly shared more and more information that was once reserved for their private domain. He said: 'In the past five or six years… people have really gotten more comfortable with sharing information… doing so more openly and with more people.'

LONDON EVENING STANDARD

I really wonder if he, and similar advocates of the erosion of privacy norms, are correct. Young people certainly do upload a lot of content on to Facebook, pictures on Flickr and video clips on YouTube that I find very surprising indeed. That might suggest, at first sight, that they are less hidebound than their parents' and grandparents' generation. They have cast off the inhibitions of previous generations.

But the youthful uploaders of risqué content often learn to regret their liberality. In a recent case before the Press Complaints Commission, a young woman objected to a magazine having published provocative pictures she had placed on Facebook, which had then been picked up and run on numerous sites across the net.

In refusing to uphold her complaint, the PCC pointed to her own complicity in compromising her privacy. Her pictures were in the public domain and, in such circumstances, it could not censure the magazine for showing to its couple of hundred thousand readers what millions across the world had already seen.

That woman, four years on from posting those pictures, certainly wishes she had not been so uninhibited and she is not alone. There have been plenty of less high-profile similar examples.

In a panel session at Google's Zeitgeist Europe 2010 conference in Hertfordshire on Monday, this dispute about where we should draw the line between the private and the public led to a clash between Sir Tim Berners-Lee, inventor of the World Wide Web, and Shami Chakrabarti, director of Liberty.

Though he did not advocate the release of personal data, his belief that as much information as possible should be available on the net spurred Chakrabarti to refer to 'the dark side' of digital advancement that allows people to forfeit their privacy.

She said: 'Civilisation requires ethics, law and humanity to temper what can be achieved by technology.' It was a case, she said, of 'we can, but should we?'.

There is much sense in what she says. But I think it's too late to erect barriers. Indeed, the whole ethos of the net is one of freedom. So, just as in the world before the Internet, people have to make up their own minds what should and should not be private.

The difference between the past and now is that a mistake is for ever. It never goes away. Ask that young woman who complained to the PCC.

19 May 2010

⇨ The above information is reprinted with kind permission from the *London Evening Standard*. Visit www.thisislondon.co.uk for more information.

Media regulation

Information from Media Wise.

Journalists are the eyes and ears of the public. In a democratic society they must be free to investigate and report matters of public concern.

And the public should be able to trust them to provide accurate information.

Many who find themselves 'in the news' are unhappy about the way their story has been presented or the way journalists have obtained information.

Regulatory bodies for the print and broadcast media receive some 10,000 complaints a year. Inaccuracy and unfairness top the list of complaints about journalism.

Many laws restrict what can be published but not the behaviour of journalists, and there are few legal remedies for inaccurate reporting.

Legal aid is not available for libel cases, which are very expensive, but it can be obtained if you are claiming that a 'malicious falsehood' has been published.

Regulatory bodies for the print and broadcast media receive some 10,000 complaints a year

There is no statutory regulation of the press. Instead there is an entirely voluntary system which does not have the force of law.

The industry has drawn up a Code of Practice and funds the Press Complaints Commission to resolve or adjudicate complaints. Editors agree to publish the PCC's criticisms, but damages cannot be awarded.

Parliament has empowered Ofcom to regulate broadcasting. They can order broadcasters to publish apologies and corrections, while serious breaches can result in fines or even the loss of a licence to broadcast.

The BBC is governed by a Royal Charter and also has its own internal regulatory system.

⇨ The above information is reprinted with kind permission from Media Wise. Visit www.mediawise. org.uk for more information.

Four years on, phone-hacking scandal is still growing

Four years ago a News of the World reporter was jailed over the hacking of celebrities' phone lines. But the scandal rumbles on, and the questions continue to multiply.

By Jamie Doward and Jenny Stevens

Four years after the phone-hacking scandal at the *News of the World* saw the newspaper's former royal correspondent, Clive Goodman, jailed, the story refuses to die.

Each week another celebrity launches a legal action against the paper, generating a fresh batch of damaging allegations that Rupert Murdoch's media empire could do without. *The Observer* has established that at least six people have issued proceedings against the paper, with potentially scores more in the pipeline.

The problems for the tabloid, however, are not confined to these cases. 11 people are taking separate legal action against Glenn Mulcaire, the private investigator at the heart of the scandal, who is appealing against a decision to make him divulge which journalists on the paper paid him to hack phones. Until this case is resolved – the court of appeal is expected to hand down a judgment in May – many outstanding issues cannot be addressed.

'It's vital that the court of appeal acts to break the logjam and holds Mulcaire's appeal immediately so this can be resolved,' said Paul Farrelly, an MP on the culture, media and sport select committee, which conducted an inquiry into the affair.

Questions have been asked about how Mulcaire is financing his appeal. News International, the Rupert Murdoch company that owns the *News of the World*, has declined to comment.

If Mulcaire were to confirm that other journalists were involved in phone hacking, serious questions would be asked about how Andy Coulson, the Prime Minister's director of communications, who was editing the newspaper at the time, could have been unaware of the practice, as he maintains. Earlier this month it emerged that the paper's news editor, Ian Edmondson, had been suspended amid allegations relating to the hacking of actress Sienna Miller's phone.

There is speculation that, if the names of other journalists on the paper were to be confirmed by Mulcaire, it would bolster claims that phone hacking by the publication's staff was systemic – something that might provide a tipping point in Coulson's career as a spin doctor.

Many close observers of the saga have long been puzzled as to why it was that only Goodman was charged. In addition to pleading guilty to hacking royal aides' phones in the original criminal trial, Mulcaire pleaded guilty to hacking the phones of five other celebrities. In his summing up of the case, Mr Justice Gross, the presiding judge, said of Mulcaire that in relation to these counts 'you had not dealt with Goodman but with others at News International'.

> **Each week another celebrity launches a legal action against the paper, generating a fresh batch of damaging allegations that Rupert Murdoch's media empire could do without**

As the culture, media and sport select committee observed, there was no further investigation of who those 'others' might be. 'We are concerned at the readiness of all of those involved – News International, the police and the PCC [Press Complaints Commission] – to leave Mr Goodman as the sole scapegoat without carrying out a full investigation at the time,' the committee inquiry concluded.

The Crown Prosecution Service explained that to have trawled all of Mulcaire's files would have made the case 'unmanageable'. The CPS said such decisions were routine 'in cases where there is a large number of potential offences' and added that 'for any potential victim not reflected in the charges actually brought, it was agreed that the police would inform them of the situation'.

But questions are being asked about whether the police informed all potential victims that they may have been targets: and, if not, why not? Some have gone as far as to suggest that, if revealed, the full extent of the hacking would jeopardise the close relationship some Scotland Yard officers have enjoyed with the *News of the World*.

A small group of suspected phone-hacking victims

THE GUARDIAN

– including Lord Prescott, the former Deputy Prime Minister, and former deputy Met police commissioner and London mayoral candidate Brian Paddick – is seeking a judicial review into Scotland Yard's handling of the investigation.

Prescott's lawyer, Tamsin Allen, believes there may have been thousands of victims. An estimated 3,000 numbers were listed in documents seized by police in 2006. Even taking into account the possibility that some victims may have had multiple phone numbers, it means there could still have been between 1,000 and 2,000 victims, something that would further undermine the *News of the World*'s claim that the hacking was the work of one rogue reporter.

'We didn't believe that there was only one rogue reporter involved,' Farrelly said. 'Now all of these civil actions are chipping away at this defence, which is completely risible.'

> ## *Prescott's lawyer, Tamsin Allen, believes there may have been thousands of victims. An estimated 3,000 numbers were listed in documents seized by police in 2006*

Far from signalling an end to the newspaper's problems, it seems Goodman's conviction was only their beginning.

16 January 2011

PCC statement on phone hacking

Information from the Press Complaints Commission.

The PCC has remained concerned about the issue of phone hacking, which raises serious questions about journalistic ethics and past conduct by journalists. Of course, the Commission cannot comment about matters that are properly being considered by police at this time. Nor can it interfere with ongoing legal actions, based on information to which we are not currently privy. However, the PCC is resolute in its determination to ensure future good practice in the industry.

On 19 January, the Commission discussed, at length, the issue of phone hacking at its monthly meeting. The Commission undertook to institute a working group, with a lay majority, to consider the new information that becomes available, and make recommendations to the Commission (which will be published). The purpose of this will be to draw together lessons learned as a result of the outcomes of the relevant police inquiries and ongoing legal actions. It will also consider the outcome of the current internal inquiry of the *News of the World*. The Committee will review the PCC's own previous actions in regard to this matter.

The Phone Hacking Review Committee will comprise the two most recent lay Commissioners (who joined after December 2009), both of whom are experts in relevant legal fields:

⇨ Ian Walden, Professor of Information and Communications Law, Queen Mary University of London.

⇨ Julie Spence, former Chief Constable, Cambridgeshire Police.

There will be one editorial Commissioner: John McLellan, the editor of the Scotsman.

It is important to make clear that phone hacking is a criminal offence, and the Commission has been consistent in its condemnation of it. It has also been consistently clear that it is not the role of the PCC (or within its powers) to duplicate the investigations of the police, or to establish criminality. However, its role is to work to raise standards in the industry, and it is committed to take this opportunity (at the conclusion of the relevant processes) to do so in this area.

31 January 2011

⇨ The above information is reprinted with kind permission from the Press Complaints Commission. Visit www.pcc.org.uk for more information.

Nick Clegg: 'Chilling' libel laws will be overhauled

Libel laws that have a 'chilling' effect on free speech and debate will be overhauled, Nick Clegg will promise today.

By James Kirkup

The Coalition will bring forward new laws to give academics, scientists and journalists greater protection from potentially ruinous legal action from people or companies who disagree with them.

The new rules will put an end to 'libel tourism', where wealthy foreigners use English courts to sue over publications in their home country, the Deputy Prime Minister will say.

In a London speech lauding the Coalition's policies to 'restore British freedoms', the Liberal Democrat leader will say that England's current libel laws are stifling free speech and informed debate.

Critics of the current laws say it is too easy for wealthy individuals and companies to launch defamation actions against people who say or write something that they do not like.

The substantial legal costs of contesting such actions in court often force writers and publishers to concede in the face of even flimsy accusations.

'It is simply not right when academics and journalists are effectively bullied into silence by the prospect of costly legal battles with wealthy individuals and big businesses,' Mr Clegg will say.

A Government Bill will be published in March setting out new protections against libel actions, and making it harder to launch such actions.

Sources said that under the Bill, existing defences including 'fair comment' will be clarified to make them stronger.

Charities, scientists and academics will also be allowed to use the public interest defence, which is currently restricted to journalists.

There will also be rules to prevent 'trivial' legal actions, which could involve companies or individuals having to show much more clearly that a report or publication has caused them personal or financial harm.

Mr Clegg will pledge that the Coalition's measures will prevent foreign claimants bringing cases against foreign defendants in the English courts when their connection with England is 'tenuous'.

'We believe claimants should not be able to threaten claims on what are essentially trivial grounds. We are going to tackle libel tourism. And we're going to look at how the law can be updated to better reflect the realities of the Internet,' Mr Clegg will say.

The new rules will put an end to 'libel tourism'

He will also commit the Coalition to addressing the high costs of defamation proceedings, reviewing 'no win – no fee' agreements that allow complainants to launch actions without immediate financial cost.

The Bill is expected to be published in draft form in March then subjected to a six-month consultation.

Lib Dem poll ratings are slumping and some members are disillusioned with the Coalition. So Mr Clegg will use his speech to argue that the Government is committed to enacting Lib Dem policies on civil liberties and personal freedom.

'People cannot be free when the state is forever on their back; when their liberties are denied and their autonomy is undermined,' he will say. 'This Government is going to restore British freedoms. It is part of our wider project to resettle the relationship between people and government.'

7 January 2011

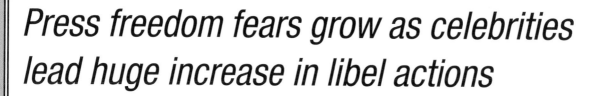

Press freedom fears grow as celebrities lead huge increase in libel actions

Libel actions brought by stars from sport and showbusiness have soared in the last two years, new figures reveal.

By Paul Cheston

The number of reported defamation cases leapt from 57 in 2007/08 to 78 the following year – a rise of 36 per cent. The figures then increased by another six per cent to 83 during 2009/10.

The jump has been led by celebrities, says legal information provider Sweet & Maxwell. Its own cases have nearly trebled from 11 in 2008/09 to 30 over the last year.

The use of privacy injunctions by celebrities is increasingly popular

The researchers attribute the rise to closer working relationships between agents and managers of celebrities and the law firms that specialise in bringing defamation claims against the media.

They also point to wider use of digital media monitoring services by stars' representatives to identify potentially damaging material.

A third factor is the growing use of 'no win no fee' agreements. These encourage defamation claims against the media which could not otherwise be afforded.

The use of privacy injunctions by celebrities against what is said and written about them is also increasingly popular.

Korieh Duodu, co-author of the latest edition of *Defamation: Law, Procedure and Practice*, says the figures for legal actions are even higher once these are taken into account.

The number of reported defamation cases leapt from 57 in 2007/08 to 78 the following year – a rise of 36 per cent. The figures then increased by another six per cent to 83 during 2009/10

The research shows that despite the overall rise in reported defamation court cases, only three in 2009/10 could be categorised 'libel tourism' by foreigners using the British legal system to sue a media outlet with few interests in the UK.

But critics say British libel law is notoriously weighted in favour of the claimant, letting powerful foreign figures use our courts for the restriction of press freedom.

The US has just passed legislation to prevent UK libel judgements being enforced there.

2 September 2010

⇨ Information from the *London Evening Standard*. Visit www.thisislondon.co.uk for more.

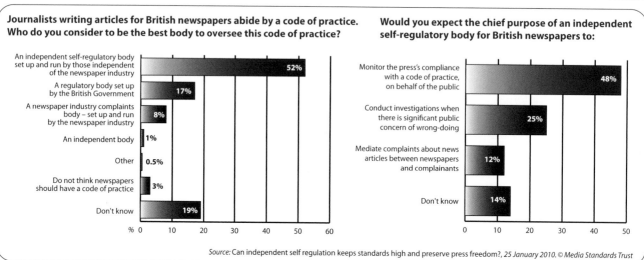

Journalists writing articles for British newspapers abide by a code of practice. Who do you consider to be the best body to oversee this code of practice?

- An independent self-regulatory body set up and run by those independent of the newspaper industry: **52%**
- A regulatory body set up by the British Government: **17%**
- A newspaper industry complaints body – set up and run by the newspaper industry: **8%**
- An independent body: **1%**
- Other: **0.5%**
- Do not think newspapers should have a code of practice: **3%**
- Don't know: **19%**

Would you expect the chief purpose of an independent self-regulatory body for British newspapers to:

- Monitor the press's compliance with a code of practice, on behalf of the public: **48%**
- Conduct investigations when there is significant public concern of wrong-doing: **25%**
- Mediate complaints about news articles between newspapers and complainants: **12%**
- Don't know: **14%**

Source: Can independent self regulation keeps standards high and preserve press freedom?, *25 January 2010.* © *Media Standards Trust*

LONDON EVENING STANDARD

Selling your story – words of warning

We all like gossip – but we don't like gossips.

People who try to make money out of something unusual that has happened to them or their friends often live to rue the day – especially if they break a confidence just to earn some extra cash.

The real victim of most 'kiss and tell' stories is the person who does the selling. Few consider the horrendous consequences which can wreck their lives and those of their friends.

Publicity-seekers cannot easily complain if their story backfires on them. By taking money they become 'fair game' in the eyes of the media.

When a publication 'buys an exclusive' it gains control of a person's life – even a good hotel loses its glamour when you are a virtual prisoner – and can run the story however and whenever it chooses.

One publication may have bought the rights to a story, but there is nothing to prevent its rivals publishing different versions of events.

Some editors may claim the public have a right to know about the story – but there is a world of difference between an item that is 'of interest to the public' and one that is 'in the public interest'.

The main reason for buying stories is to increase the sales of a publication. The feelings of the people involved in the story take second place to the commercial aims of the publisher.

Think twice and take advice

If you are tempted to make money by selling your story, get professional advice FIRST and consider the long-term consequences for you and your family.

MediaWise advises people NOT to auction their story to the highest bidder. It could cost them their friends, and their peace of mind.

Don't court prosecution

If you supply information that is defamatory you could find yourself open to a libel action.

If you are a potential witness in a court case there are special risks in selling your version of events. It could even contribute to a miscarriage of justice. Your credibility may be challenged in court, especially if you have been offered a bonus related to the verdict.

Better be safe than sorry

If you have information you believe should be published in the public interest, it is better to manage the release of that information rather than risk your self-respect by auctioning it.

The best course of action would be to work with a trustworthy journalist, a solicitor, or even a PR company, having first agreed the terms of the arrangement. They can help organise a press conference, negotiate a fair price and provide protection from media exploitation.

If you want to remain anonymous, documentary evidence can always be supplied to journalists in a plain envelope.

⇨ The above information is reprinted with kind permission from MediaWise. Visit their website at www.mediawise.org.uk for more information on this and other related topics.

MEDIAWISE

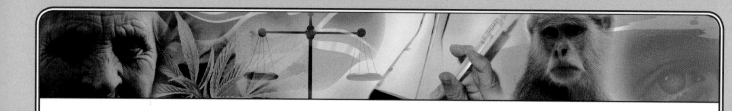

⇨ The UK is effectively saturated with traditional electronic media: multi-television, multi-radio and multi-telephone households are commonplace. (page 1)

⇨ The printed press is commonly divided into three sectors – 'quality', 'middle market' and 'red-top tabloid'. For more than 20 years, all the papers in the latter two categories have been tabloid in size. (page 2)

⇨ UK television channels broadcast about 2.5 million hours of programming a year. There are four main public service free-to-air broadcasters. (page 3)

⇨ According to a recent IPA survey, people watch 3.7 hours of television per day, listen to the radio for 2.1 hours and access the Internet for 1.8 hours per day. (page 4)

⇨ 35% of all adults claim to use Facebook each week – up from 16% in 2008. For 15-24s, Facebook's weekly reach is 79% – up from 39% in 2008. (page 5)

⇨ Only 24% of the people heard or read about in print, radio and television news are female. In contrast, 76% – more than three out of four – of the people in the news are male. (page 6)

⇨ The growing popularity of smartphones – and the changing way we use our mobiles – is increasing our overall use of communications, and helping us do much more simultaneously. (page 10)

⇨ Over two-thirds (67 per cent) of the time that younger people spend on the Internet on a computer is spent communicating with other people, comprised of 29 per cent social networking, 19 per cent email and 19 per cent instant messaging. (page 11)

⇨ The UK saw the highest growth in smartphone take-up in the past year, with a 70 per cent rise in subscriber numbers between January 2009 and January 2010. (page 13)

⇨ Despite super-fast broadband being available in some parts of the comparator countries, fewer than one in 50 households in the UK, France, Italy, Germany and Spain had a superfast broadband connection at the end of 2009. (page 15)

⇨ More than 100 million people joined microblogging service Twitter this year, the company has revealed. (page 18)

⇨ WikiLeaks is a website set up by a group of human rights activists, technical people and journalists to bring sensitive materials to the attention of the public. (page 20)

⇨ WikiLeaks sometimes does not know its source for reasons of security – it instead goes to the area the document covers to try and verify the document itself. (page 22)

⇨ Ofcom's powers include fining media organisations for breaching regulations and closing down illegal 'pirate' broadcasters (and even commercial broadcasters). (page 27)

⇨ According to the opinion survey conducted for the submission, the public prefers an independent self-regulatory body (52%) to a newspaper industry complaints body (8%) or a regulatory body set up by the government (17%). (page 29)

⇨ Facebook Inc. now has more than 400 million active users globally, a massive 229% increase from a year ago. (page 30)

⇨ Regulatory bodies for the print & broadcast media receive some 10,000 complaints a year. Inaccuracy and unfairness top the list of complaints about journalism. (page 34)

⇨ The BBC is governed by a Royal Charter and also has its own internal regulatory system. (page 34)

⇨ Critics say British libel law is notoriously weighted in favour of the claimant, letting powerful foreign figures use our courts for the restriction of press freedom. (page 38)

BBC

The British Broadcasting Corporation. The BBC is the largest public broadcasting service in the world. It is funded by a licence fee paid by UK households and provides extensive TV, radio and online services.

Blog

A website which features individual writers' or groups of writers' personal discourse (similar to a journal), sharing ideas, information, opinions and observations. Entries are added regularly and may feature photos, videos and interactive comments left by readers.

The Editor's Code of Practice

The code of practice by which journalists, publishers and editors must abide. The Editor's Code aims to protect the rights of individuals as well as the public's right to information. It includes guidance on areas such as press accuracy, individuals' right to privacy, harassment by journalists, intrusion into grief or shock and discrimination. It is applicable to both printed and online editorial content.

Freedom of expression/freedom of speech

Being able to speak without censorship. In the context of the media, this also refers to the ability to publish information, opinions and ideas without restriction. It is considered a fundamental human right to have freedom of expression. This right is recognised under Article 19 of the Universal Declaration of Human Rights.

Libel

A published statement about an individual which is untrue and may damage their reputation. Libel can refer to the printed word or pictures.

Ofcom

The independent regulator for all radio, television and telecom broadcasting in the UK. Ofcom deal with all consumer complaints regarding television or radio, issue broadcasting licences and promote competition. Ofcom are Government-approved and act under the Communications Act 2003.

Press Complaints Commission (PCC)

The independent body who monitor the self-regulation of the UK press. The Press Complaints Commission deals with complaints about the press, guided by the Editor's Code of Practice. The PCC has no legal power as such: newspapers and magazines voluntarily adhere to the regulation.

Print media

Traditional hard-copy media such as newspapers and magazines.

Reality TV

A genre of television that has become highly popular in recent years, with the aim of documenting 'real' life with 'real' people rather than professional actors. Although unscripted, reality TV situations are often carefully structured by the programme makers. Examples include *Big Brother* and *The X Factor*.

Smartphone

A mobile device with advanced capabilities, much like a handheld computer. One popular example is the Apple iPhone. They are increasingly being used to access the Internet and may have other features such as a camera, GPS and MP3 player.

Social media

Media which are designed specifically for electronic communication. 'Social networking' websites allow users to interact using instant messaging, share information, photos and videos and ultimately create an online community. Examples include Facebook, LinkedIn and micro-blogging site Twitter.

WikiLeaks

WikiLeaks is a controversial website which publishes sensitive information from anonymous sources it believes to be in the public interest. It has leaked information from many sources which are not normally available for public view, including confidential political documents. The website was set up by Australian hacker Julian Assange.

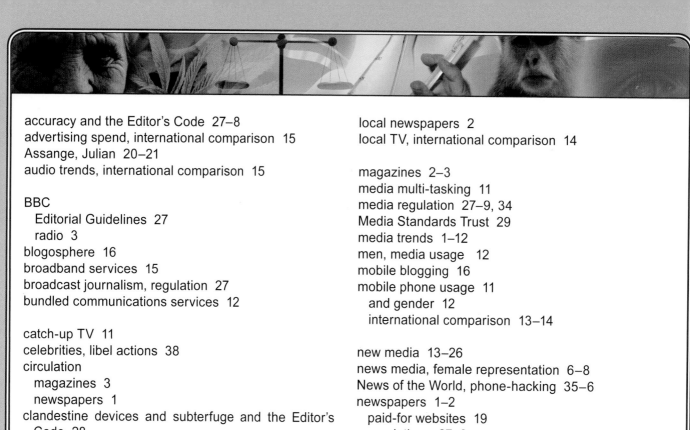

ACKNOWLEDGEMENTS

The publisher is grateful for permission to reproduce the following material.

While every care has been taken to trace and acknowledge copyright, the publisher tenders its apology for any accidental infringement or where copyright has proved untraceable. The publisher would be pleased to come to a suitable arrangement in any such case with the rightful owner.

Chapter One: Media Trends

The UK's media landscape, © European Journalism Centre, Media and communication trends, © IPA, Who makes the news?, © World Association for Christian Communication, Negative effects of media/entertainment upon teens, © Child.net, Real life vs reality TV, © Psychologies, TV, phones and Internet take up almost half of our waking hours, © Ofcom.

Chapter Two: New Media

UK consumers revealed as early adopters of new technology, © Ofcom, State of the blogosphere 2010, © Technorati.com, Reality TV and Facebook – the worst innovations of the last decade, © Telegraph Media Group Limited 2010, Twitter adds 100 million new users in 2010, © Telegraph Media Group Limited 2010, Websites and iPads – which way now for newspapers?, © Media UK, What is WikiLeaks?, © Channel 4, Traditional papers didn't know how to handle WikiLeaks, © Guardian News and Media Limited 2010, Freedom of Information in the WikiLeaks era, © Judith Townend.

Chapter Three: Media Regulations and Privacy

Regulation and self-regulation of the media, © In Brief, Major reform of Press Complaints Commission proposed, © Media Standards Trust, Security-related social networking issues abound in organisations, © Search Security, Reuters sets up social media guidelines, © Guardian News and Media Limited 2010, Just what is privacy in the era of Google and Facebook?, © 2011 ES London Limited, Media regulation, © MediaWise, Four years on, phone-hacking scandal is still growing, © Guardian News and Media Limited 2010, PCC statement on phone hacking, © Press Complaints Commission, Nick Clegg: 'Chilling' libel laws will be overhauled, © Telegraph Media Group Limited 2010, Press freedom fears grow as celebrities lead huge increase in libel actions, © 2011 ES London, Selling your story – words of warning, © MediaWise.

Illustrations

Pages 2, 19, 24, 37: Angelo Madrid; pages 6, 20, 28, 32: Simon Kneebone; pages 18, 26, 36, 39: Don Hatcher; pages 12, 30: Bev Aisbett.

Cover photography

Left: © Michael W. Centre: © Ilker. Right: © bizior photography – www.bizior.com.

Additional acknowledgements

Research by Rebecca Kirby.

Editorial by Carolyn Kirby on behalf of Independence.

And with thanks to the Independence team: Mary Chapman, Sandra Dennis and Jan Sunderland.

Lisa Firth
Cambridge
April, 2011

ASSIGNMENTS

The following tasks aim to help you think through the issues surrounding the media debate and provide a better understanding of the topic.

1 Read *Media and communication trends* on page 4. Carry out a survey amongst your friends and family to find out how much television they watch on average per day. Aim to include at least six respondents in your survey. Do they follow national trends? Write a short report on your findings.

2 Read *Who makes the news?* on page 6. Choose a television news broadcast and aim to listen to it for three consecutive days. Do you notice a pattern in the gender of the reporters? Or of the subjects of news stories? Do you think that a gender imbalance in the news is noticeable? Discuss your findings with your classmates.

3 Aim to spend one day without new media in your life. Try not to text, phone, watch television or use the Internet for a whole day. Was it as hard as you thought? What did you do to fill the time you usually spend using media? Did it surprise you the extent to which you rely on it? Write an account of your day.

4 Find reports in two different newspapers – a broadsheet and a tabloid – covering the same story. In pairs, analyse the way the story is reported, including which facts are given, how people are described and the language used. How do the articles differ?

5 What are the most popular UK-based blogs? Visit one of them and write a review. What does the blogger choose to write about? What are his or her motives for blogging? Why is the blog so popular? Do you think it is valuable – would you read more?

6 Hold a debate on the advantages and disadvantages of social networking. What benefits, if any, do you think websites such as Facebook and Twitter bring to society? What drawbacks might they have?

7 Read *What is WikiLeaks?* on page 20. Give a short presentation to your class explaining what WikiLeaks is and discussing the ethical arguments surrounding the release of sensitive information. Try to outline the controversial debate between issues such as national security versus freedom of information. Finish your presentation with the question 'Is WikiLeaks doing more harm than good?' What are your classmates' reactions?

8 'This house believes that the Press Complaints Commission is a "toothless tiger" which is entirely ineffective as a regulatory body for the UK press.' Debate this motion in two groups, with one arguing in favour and the other against. Prepare by doing some research into specific cases dealt with by the PCC.

9 Using the Internet, carry out research into the circulation figures of two different newspapers. Compare your findings and display them in a set of graphs.

10 Ofcom regulate all radio and television broadcasting in the UK. Visit their website at www.ofcom.org.uk to find out more about how the regulations are enforced and how you would go about making a complaint. Print journalism has no equivalent regulatory body. Do you think this is right? Do you think self-regulation is an appropriate control for UK newspapers and magazines? Discuss your views in groups of four, then present your conclusions to the rest of your class.

11 Design a poster warning people of the dangers of selling their story to the press. Try to make the potential dangers of publicity clear to readers, including what consequences they might have to face.

12 Write a news report on phone hacking by journalists. Research the issue of phone hacking using Internet and newspapers, and try to work out what is fact and what is opinion. Collate the information that you want to include and write a short article suitable for a student newspaper.

13 Read *Nick Clegg: 'Chilling' libel laws will be overhauled* on page 37 and *Press freedom fears grow as celebrities lead huge increase in libel actions* on page 38. Role play the court case of a journalist who is being prosecuted for libel. Students acting as the Defence could use arguments such as freedom of information, whilst the Prosecution could accuse the journalist of invasion of privacy. What do your jury decide?